T0314762

Weeding
and Maintenance
of Reference Collections

Sydney J. Pierce
Editor

School of Library and Information Studies
The University of Oklahoma

Routledge
Taylor & Francis Group

NEW YORK AND LONDON

First Published by

The Haworth Press, Inc., 10 Alice Street, Binghamton, NY 13904-1580
EUROSPAN/Haworth, 3 Henrietta Street, London WC2E 8LU England

This edition published 2011 by Routledge
711 Third Avenue, New York, NY 10017
2 Park Square, Milton Park, Abingdon, Oxon, OX14 4RN

Weeding and Maintenance of Reference Collections has also been published as *The Reference Librarian*, Number 29 1990.

Library of Congress Cataloging-in-Publication Data

Weeding and maintenance of reference collections / Sydney J. Pierce, editor.
      P.   cm.
   Published also as v. 29 of the Reference librarian.
   Includes bibliographical references.
   ISBN 1-56024-001-6 (alk. paper) : ISBN 1-56024-976-5 (pbk. : alk paper).
      1. Reference services (Libraries). 2. Libraries—Special collections—Reference books. 3. Reference books—Bibliography—Methodology. 4. Discarding of books, periodicals, etc. 5. Collection development (Libraries) I. Pierce, Sydney J.
   Z711.QW4   1990
   025.2'16—dc20   90-30910
                                                                             CIP

Publisher's Note
The publisher has gone to great lengths to ensure the quality of this reprint but points out that some imperfections in the original may be apparent.

Weeding and Maintenance of Reference Collections

Forthcoming topics in *The Reference Librarian* series:

* Continuing Education of Reference Librarians, Number 30
* The Reference Library User: Problems and Solutions, Number 31
* Government Documents and Reference Services, Number 32
* The Bright Side of Reference Services, Number 33

Published:

Weeding and Maintenance
of Reference Collections

CONTENTS

II. MAKING POLICY DECISIONS

III. EVALUATING AND WEEDING COLLECTIONS

ABOUT THE EDITOR

Sydney J. Pierce, PhD, MLS, is a professor at the School of Library and Information Studies of the University of Oklahoma. She has taught library school courses in reference and collection development at Emory University, Indiana University, UCLA, and, as a Fulbright lecturer, at the Federal University of Minas Gerais in Brazil. She has also worked in reference in academic and public libraries. Dr. Pierce is a member of the American Library Association, the Society for Social Studies of Science, and the Association for Library and Information Science Education.

Introduction

Sydney J. Pierce

Libraries often neglect their reference collections until faced with a space or budget crisis. New reference works are acquired enthusiastically, but librarians approach evaluating and weeding what is already on the shelves with great caution. As a result, older works may remain in reference indefinitely, in spite of low user interest and increasingly dated content. When shortages of space or budget finally force a reduction in the size of the collection, they may inspire desperate and ill-thought-out measures, with materials weeded according to space available on the shelf, and standing orders considered for cancellation on the basis of price alone.

Our reference collections need better management. Unplanned collection development and a neglect of weeding impair the efficiency of reference service long before they lead to space and budget problems. Good reference work requires reference collections in which the coverage of subjects is known and predictable, sources are easily located, and the type of information provided corresponds to user needs. As unplanned and unweeded collections grow, shelf and seating space shrink, and works with needed information are lost in the clutter of outdated and inappropriate materials crowding the shelves. Weeding and cancellation of standing orders without careful attention to collection balance and user needs only makes the situation worse.

Most librarians receive little preparation for evaluating and weeding reference collections in library school and the library literature

Sydney J. Pierce was teaching in the UCLA Graduate School of Library and Information Science when this volume was prepared for publication. At present, she is a member of the faculty of the School of Library and Information Studies, University of Oklahoma, 401 West Brooks, Room 120, Norman, OK 73019.

1

gives little useful advice. We place too much emphasis on selecting and evaluating new works to be added to the collection, and not enough on evaluating the result and selecting material for weeding. This volume of *The Reference Librarian* was planned to remedy this, offering practical advice to those confronting the need to evaluate their collections and establish better collection management policies and procedures. Most authors are reference or collection development librarians drawing on their own experience in the area. Others are researchers investigating the way different libraries deal with problems.

The articles in this volume have been divided into separate groups dealing with institutional contexts, policy decisions, and programs for evaluation and weeding. Most articles, however, consider a broader range of concerns than might be suggested by the section in which they are placed, dealing with questions of general interest to any reference librarian.

CONSIDERING THE INSTITUTIONAL CONTEXT

Since library schools rely heavily on academic libraries and academic librarians contribute heavily to the library literature, large academic library reference collections often become our models of what reference collections ought to look like. But the reference departments of different types of libraries have different users and different service objectives. Even within libraries of the same type, users and objectives may differ. Kroll begins this section with a discussion of the importance of institutional objectives in planning more effective information services, using as an example the implications for user services of decisions made on the formats to be represented in the reference collection.

The remaining three articles in the first section discuss problems of reference collection development in different types of libraries. O'Connor and Dyer describe the ways in which traditional approaches to reference collection management are inappropriate in a corporate library, suggesting that traditional approaches encourage librarians to ignore both use and users and raising some fundamental philosophical questions of concern to other types of libraries as well. Goodwin, Patrick, and Pringle describe reference collection management in a public library system striving to distribute information resources more equitably among geographically dispersed users, as well as describing a plan for reducing the time needed to select new reference works. Tezla discusses the use of the RLG Conspectus as an approach to the evaluation of an academic library reference collection, emphasizing the need to coordinate development of reference and circulating collections.

Most articles in the volume in some way demonstrate the importance of institutional environments. Though most take what is described as an approach based on user needs, the term has different meanings in different institutional contexts. This can be seen in different attitudes toward duplication of sources. Goodwin, Patrick, and Pringle take duplication for granted. It serves public library user needs by making similar resources available to individuals using different branches, though the number of sources available is more limited than could be provided if the same funding were used to build a large central collection. Academic libraries tend to take the opposite approach, avoiding duplication even when this results in unequal access for some groups of users. Waters, for example, describes standing order cancellations that remove needed sources from some branches of the library, and Harloe and Barber suggest that users at some locations be furnished with superseded editions of frequently published sources. Many academic librarians feel that the needs of their users, given a high priority on the encouragement of research, are best served by providing greater numbers of sources on highly specialized topics, even though this may mean providing fewer duplicates in convenient locations. All libraries consider user needs, but what needs-based decision-making involves depends on their institutional objectives.

Even where user needs are similar, libraries in different institutional contexts may seek different solutions to similar problems. Corporate and public libraries, for example, frequently use circulating materials to answer reference questions instead of building the very large reference collections usually maintained by academic libraries. O'Connor and Dyer suggest that corporate libraries reduce the number of works placed in reference to a minimum. Goodwin, Patrick, and Pringle suggest that small public libraries interfile reference materials with the circulating collection. Both practices encourage heavier use of the circulating collection. Reference librarians need to be willing to consider alternatives and select the approaches that seem best to further the institutional objectives they are striving to meet.

MAKING POLICY DECISIONS

In general, developing a reference collection development policy requires decisions in three general areas. First, reference librarians must identify the objectives to be met by the collection — for what purpose are materials placed in reference, and what needs of librarians and users should the reference collection be designed to meet? Second, they must define the collection's content — the nature and organization of different parts of the collection, the criteria for placing materials in each part, and the formats and degree of duplication desired for reference materials. Third, they must work with other departments to develop procedures — the means through which sources are added to or removed from the reference collection, the division of workload and responsibilities among the departments concerned, and the priorities governing work on the reference collection.

Written collection development policies both relate collection management decisions to institutional objectives and provide staff with the information necessary to make and to explain these decisions. Developing such policies also encourages reference librarians to adopt good management practices early enough to serve as preventative measures. As both Kroll and Engeldinger point out, implementing policies before problems arise may help reference librarians remain in control of collection development by encouraging weeding before space becomes a problem and identifying unneeded standing orders before the serials budget cuts too deeply into the library's discretionary book funds.

In spite of this, many libraries still lack reference collection policies. Truett, in the first article in this section, reports results of a survey she made of several academic and public librarians, inquiring about policies and procedures for reference collection development. She covers problems from selection of materials through evaluation and weeding, and finds not only that written policies are rare, but also that most libraries cannot provide even basic statistics on reference collection size and the rate at which works are added and weeded.

Other articles in this section deal with specific areas in which policy decisions must be made. Futas and Tryon investigate the frequency with which public and academic libraries replace sources that appear regularly in new editions, describing criteria established both by type of source and for specific titles. Popp and Kabir alert librarians to the implications of adding large numbers of sources in CD-ROM formats to reference collections. Their article can be used as a checklist of the policy decisions and institutional adjustments that reference departments should be prepared to make before investing heavily in CD-ROM sources. Waters describes the response of a large research library's reference department to problems caused by budget reductions and by a lack of space for expansion, problems common to many libraries as they enter the 1990s.

Many articles in other sections of this volume also deal with policy issues. Some question basic assumptions made in placing materials in reference collections. Mathews and Tyckoson point out the contradictions implicit in claiming that reference collections are collections of works needed to answer reference questions, but automatically placing all materials published in "reference book" formats in the reference collection. Engeldinger demonstrates that though we often justify placing materials in reference on the basis of expected heavy use, most reference works are used infrequently, if at all.

Other articles point out problems in developing policies and procedures, especially those involving the coordination of the work of the different departments of the library involved in reference collection development. Tezla, for example, discusses the necessity of coordinating work done on the reference and the circulating collections. Weeding reference books places an unwelcome burden on technical services, and both Vincent and Harloe and Barber discuss the communication and workload problems that must be resolved before work can be expected to go smoothly.

EVALUATING AND WEEDING COLLECTIONS

Evaluation and weeding are essential to reference collection management. They are also the aspects of collection management most likely to be neglected by reference librarians. One reason for this is that librarians find it difficult to predict what reference works are likely to be needed in the future. When circulating collections are evaluated, we frequently use past circulation to predict future use. But identifying what reference sources have been used in the past is difficult, since there are no circulation records to provide records of this use. Many libraries have found no better way to determine what reference works are used than to ask reference librarians for their (often highly subjective) impressions.

The first two articles in this section therefore deal with measuring the use of reference materials. Biggs describes a variety of different methods librarians can use to determine the use materials receive, with the advantages and shortcomings of each. Engeldinger discusses the problem and describes a five-year use study of an academic library reference collection that illustrates his point that most sources do not receive enough use to justify their places on reference shelves.

The remaining three articles are practical guides to weeding reference collections. Mathews and Tyckoson provide a good general overview of the process and procedures. Vincent's humorously written "how-to" contains both good general advice and a description of the often unanticipated pitfalls encountered in weeding reference. Harloe and Barber provide a useful series of checklists of points to be considered and policy decisions to be made before embarking on any extensive weeding project.

OTHER ISSUES IN COLLECTION MANAGEMENT

In spite of the cooperation of an experienced and talented group of contributors (to whom the editor is exceedingly grateful), this volume is unbalanced and incomplete in its coverage of reference collection management. Selection of materials was excluded, since it is amply covered elsewhere. No contributors could be located for articles on some topics—most notably the concerns of school libraries and the care and preservation of reference materials—and the original list of those invited to contribute was more evenly balanced by type of library than may be obvious in the final result. As a result, some important matters are left unexplored.

The subject of the volume may in itself encourage too narrow a view of a more general problem. Both Kroll and O'Connor and

Dyer remind us that focussing on the development of the reference collection limits our options by encouraging us to think in terms of acquisition and ownership of material, when it is provision of information, not its ownership, that should be our ultimate objective. Cooperation among libraries might, for example, make it possible for research libraries to cancel standing orders for some highly specialized sources infrequently needed by researchers in order to duplicate some sources in great demand by larger numbers of users. Smaller libraries of course are already accustomed to relying on others, referring information requests to libraries that have a greater variety of reference sources on their shelves. Since articles in this volume tend to focus on the internal workings of individual libraries, cooperation is not much discussed, but it should be considered in most libraries' plans for development of their reference collections.

The arrangement of reference collections is another matter that is barely touched upon here. Libraries face several such decisions. One is the choice between maintaining a comprehensive general collection and building several smaller specialized ones. Both academic and public libraries often choose strong central reference collections as a way of giving their users access to the full range of available sources in one place. This is an excellent idea if the library's users are willing to use these strong central collections. But many library users persist in depending on collections that are conveniently located even when more distant ones would better serve their needs. Libraries trying to accommodate themselves to the needs of such users instead divide their reference sources into separate collections on subjects of interest to different populations of users — trying to place sources in the location most likely to be used by those with the greatest need of them. Neither arrangement is wholly satisfactory, but local policies on the content of different branch collections all too often seem to be based more on space and tradition than on a careful consideration of institutional objectives and the needs of local user populations.

Even less thought seems to go into justifying the internal arrangement of reference collections. Such arrangements cause more user frustration than many of us are willing to admit. Many of us have tales to tell of the barriers to use we encountered while students in library school, but few of us see the problems we ourselves are causing for users in our own libraries. Librarians too easily take for granted the existence of "ready reference" collections and special areas for such sources as encyclopedias or business sources. While considering criteria for placing works in reference, reference librarians should seek to do the same for "ready reference" and other special subdivisions of the reference collection. What justifies the separation from the rest of the reference collection? What format, content, or level of use is the criterion for placement in each special collection? How are our users alerted to the location of works in such collections? What can be done to prevent inconvenience to the user who is ignorant of the location and content of collections in special areas, or is too intimidated (e.g., by "ready reference" collections placed at or behind the reference desk) to use them? Perhaps a reconsideration of library objectives and user needs could alleviate some of the problems associated with such collections.

But the decisions to be made in the management of reference collections are too varied for coverage here. It is hoped that this volume will at least give librarians trying to deal more systematically with reference collections a place to start, and those already actively involved in the collections management process a few additional issues and ideas to consider.

I. CONSIDERING
THE INSTITUTIONAL CONTEXT

The Responsive Reference Collection: Planning for Service versus Self-Service in the Reference Area

H. Rebecca Kroll

SUMMARY. This paper discusses the need for both continuity and flexibility in reference collection building, and proposes three criteria on which to base decisions about the collection: does any prospective addition help to meet the goals of the library's parent institution, and of the library itself, and does it satisfy the specific needs of the library's particular clientele? Before adding to the collection, reference librarians should consider the subject covered, the level of coverage given, and the format in which the source is published: do all three meet the needs of the library? The paper discusses four formats in which reference sources are now published, comparing their relative strengths and weaknesses in relation to the need for service or self-service in the reference area.

INTRODUCTION

The purpose of the reference collection is to provide access to information, whether the actual sources tapped are located on the

H. Rebecca Kroll is a reference librarian who has worked at State University of New York at Buffalo and at Northwestern University Library. Correspondence may be sent to 3302 Bordero Lane, Thousand Oaks, CA 91362.

premises or out of the country. To do this effectively, the reference collection must be not only comprehensive and up to date, but also responsive to the needs of the users, requiring a combination of continuity and flexibility which is extremely difficult to maintain. The reference collection is one of the most visible parts of the library—the first place many users come and the gateway to the broad array of information available in the rest of the building and beyond. Today we have the luxury of choosing how much of this critically important area should be designed for service-oriented reference requiring a high degree of interaction between librarians and patrons, and how much should be oriented toward independent research by the library user without the need for staff intervention.

In an ideal situation, collection decisions of this nature would always be made based on a well-defined philosophy of service which could be used as a touchstone to evaluate present and possible future parts of the reference collection. The unfortunate truth, however, is that all too often the factors which determine day to day collection decisions are far from ideal, and the first of these, of course, is money. Gone from most libraries are the days when a budget for reference materials was submitted from the bottom up based on painstaking assessments of the needs of the collection; instead, most budgets are handed down from the top, based not on what is needed, but on what is available. While it should strengthen and support the library as a whole, all too often the reference collection appears to become a separate entity with a personality of its own, looming over the rest of the library, requiring more and more money, space and time to maintain. Trying to meet the seemingly insatiable demands of the reference collections while doing justice to the rest of the library can lead to severe conflicts, of which some can be settle amicably around a conference table, while others seem more suited to pistols at dawn in the staff parking lot. The major decisions today center not on what to acquire, but on what to eliminate next, as we struggle with rising subscription prices and increasingly bulky publications while trying to keep up with astounding amounts of new information.

Another unpalatable truth is that in many reference collections, history and tradition play important roles in selection decisions to the detriment of flexibility and innovation. Anything from the split between monograph and serial allocations to the location of the reference room may have become as though engraved in stone after many years, and nothing short of a major upheaval changes the situation.

A third factor which controls reference collection evaluation and evolution is influence: whether from the friends of the library, the academic library committee, the trustees or the head office, there is always at least one individual or group which exerts an unusually strong influence on internal library decisions. In some cases these groups may give invaluable help and support by representing the needs of the library's clients as a whole, but there is also the danger that a particular interest group which is far from representative will be more vocal than the rest, with the result that a biased user profile will emerge which affects collection decisions. Part of the library's juggling act is to identify and satisfy, as far as possible, these special interests without detracting from the services and materials provided for the mainstream of its clientele.

In an effort to provide a logical method of evaluating both the existing collection and potential additions to it, we need a framework on which to build so that each decision can be made in the overall context of the library's ongoing plans, rather than treated as a separate problem. To do this, we need a set of criteria for defining the reference collection. As a basis for discussion, there are three factors which should be kept in mind in the evaluation of reference material: (1) the goals of the institution served by the library, (2) the goals of the library itself, and (3) the needs and desires of the library's clientele.

A FRAMEWORK FOR CONTINUITY

On the theory that without the parent institution behind the library, be it a university, public school, county or corporation, there would be no library collection to evaluate, the first criterion for measuring any part of the collection should be how well it supports the goals of that institution. The needs of a corporation with an emphasis on technical expertise in engineering, market strategy and competitive analysis are far removed from those of a large university which places an emphasis on the social sciences, law and medicine. Whether planning and starting up a reference collection in a fresh location for a new company or school (a situation which for the most of us borders on sheer fantasy), or evaluating an existing collection badly in need of weeding and renovation, the first point of reference should be the parent institution. Like any other segment of the library, the reference collection needs to have a written policy which spells out in as explicit detail as possible how the collection will support the long-term goals of its founding entity.

Next after the institution's goals should come those of the library itself, though these two may not be synonymous. In times of shrinking budgets, many libraries enter into cooperative collection agreements which necessitate collecting in subject areas or on levels which are not required solely to support the parent institution, but which guarantee patrons access to quality collections in other areas. In addition to supporting the goals of education and research, a university library may have the further aim of turning out graduates who are knowledgeable enough to be able to function comfortably in any research library setting they may encounter in future work or study situations; rather than planning simply to provide current and comprehensive information each time a question is asked, that library may also choose to educate its users so that they are capable of finding their own answers in the future. A corporate information center, on the other hand, may have as its primary goal to supply any and all information required as quickly and accurately as possible without management ever needing to be aware of the exact methods used to obtain that information.

A final factor which should influence the definition of the reference collection is the needs and desires of the actual users who make up the library's clientele. A library which does a high turnover trade in information where there are few repeat visits will have a different client profile than one where a small group of steady users patronizes the collection on an ongoing basis, just as a private library in a commercial setting will operate differently from a public library which needs to be constantly on the lookout for outside funding and support. In the one case, user education is less important than efficiency of response; in the other, the ease with which the user can become comfortable with the structure of the collection and its access points may be a primary concern. In this context, "needs" and "desires" may be in exact opposition: the greatest *desire* of many undergraduate students is to have all the requisite information for term papers supplied to them on demand, preferably in a format requiring little rewriting, whereas their greatest *need* may be to learn how to use the reference tools themselves to help them through the next four years of research papers and on to graduate school. Whether or not the reference librarian should be the one to determine what is best for the student in this context is a question which affects the subject makeup of the collection less than it affects the formats chosen; in all the examples given, the use to which reference materials will be put, and by whom, will have an impact on the service/self-service ratio. The important point for our purposes here is that there are three major factors which should constitute the point of departure for a reference collection policy.

CRITERIA FOR EVALUATION

Given that the background has been established for evaluating and updating the reference collection, how does one approach the actual evaluation itself? Rather than attacking the shelves and discarding material based on date of publication or currency alone in an attempt to update reference holdings, most libraries establish a set of guidelines ahead of time which will forestall many arguments, outlining the subject areas to be covered along with the level of coverage each subject receives. An undergraduate library will not collect in the same depth as a graduate research library, while the technical library may have an astounding degree of coverage in two or three areas but be rightfully sparse in peripheral subjects.

Subject and level have long been standard ways of defining collection policy, but it is time to include a new dimension also: the format in which materials will be purchased. In order to be truly responsive to the needs of its clientele, today's library needs to be flexible in form as well as subject content. Never before have we been faced with such diversity in our reference tools; each has its place, but deciding which will work best in any given situation is not easy. Is there such a thing as the ideal mix of formats for the reference collection? Consider that we have at least four major forms of reference materials available now: paper, microform, online and optical disc—sometimes for the same product line!

FLEXIBILITY AND FORMAT

Taking these in their chronological order of development, we can briefly review the strengths and weaknesses of each. Traditional paper reference materials are normally the most straightforward to use, usually have instructions included for self-help, and can accommodate more than one user at a time in the case of multi-volume sets. Their costs are predictable, at least in the short term, there are few access costs except basic processing and possibly binding, and the staff time needed to introduce new users to the paper part of the reference collection can be estimated from experience. On the other hand, printed sources consume a great deal of space, tend to contain less recent information than is available in other formats, and do increase dramatically in price on an all too regular basis. They also permit only the most simple search strategies, since single terms with subheadings are the only access available.

Microform sources take considerably less space, may be updated more frequently than their paper counterparts, although this is not always the case, and can represent a considerable savings. They also, however, have their drawbacks: equipment costs and maintenance, more patron orientation time, perceived inconvenience for patrons compared to open shelves, and usually a one-at-a-time access limitation for each title, and possibly for many microform titles, depending on the amount of equipment available. Since microform sources are simply a reproduction or an alternate form of print sources, the search strategies used can be no more complex than for their paper counterparts.

Online reference sources take a quantum leap in both costs and benefits: they provide the most recent possible information, and they allow the greatest flexibility and complexity of search strategies. They are also, of course, usually expensive by comparison, their costs are unpredictable since they vary with the volume of use, and access is limited by the number of terminals and/or the number of staff available to work on a problem. To do really good research using most online data bases requires special training, although the menu-driven, "user-friendly" services permit researchers to perform less elegant but still successful searches for themselves without librarians as intermediaries. Even the non-menu formats of the databases can be searched successfully by someone who is familiar with a vendor's general format, although some of the fine points may be lost for any given database. The costs of searching may or may not be recovered from the patron, depending on the library's budget and philosophy of service.

Optical disc, the most recent entry into the fray, combines many of the advantages and disadvantages of all the other formats. It is extremely expensive, but the costs are once again predictable in the short term. It is capable of allowing complex search strategies by combining large numbers of terms, although not all optical disc sources make use of this strength. Both the large discs and CD-ROM discs can store very large amounts of information (CD-ROM discs can store the equivalent of over 300,000 pages of text,[1] while the larger twelve-inch discs can store twice that amount).[2] The drawback to this is that some optical systems take an extremely long time to execute a search, especially those which tag information in such a way that the entire disc must be checked again when it is time to combine sets of information or organize the data before printing.

Ease of use of optical discs by patrons varies from the ability to walk up to a terminal for the first time and perform a successful search immediately, to needing to study a manual or learn one's way around the data base by trial and error. Some of the most powerful tools are the most frustrating to work with: some allow the researcher space for making private notes which can be stored along with the search results and taken away on a separate floppy disk, but the instructions for use are frequently obscure, to put it mildly. This in turn means that there may be a very heavy demand on reference staff time to present and explain each new database; unlike printed Wilson indexes, just because you have mastered one does not mean you can now search all of them with no trouble. The information may be very up-to-date or badly out of date, depending on the publication schedule: a CD-ROM database which is updated twice a year may actually be less current than a printed source with weekly updating pamphlets, although it is certainly less exasperating to use and maintain.

Perhaps the biggest area of frustration in dealing with optical disc databases is the lack of compatibility of the equipment required: despite many attempts to establish guidelines, the various vendors have yet to cooperate to the extent of allowing one brand of reader to work for all discs, with the result that a library with a wide variety of optical disc sources usually also invests in a wide variety of equipment to mount them. Whereas any PC or compatible with a modem can access online databases, not all CD-ROM readers will access all CD-ROM databases. This means that the shelving space saved by cancelling paper subscriptions must be converted to workspace for computer equipment, readers and printers, at a much higher overall cost to the library.

There is also a security problem associated with CD-ROM in particular, since it is possible to walk off with a major helping of information tucked casually into a pocket. At the present time, few individuals have the home or office equipment on hand to make use of CD-ROM discs away from the library, but this will change with time. Already the equipment to read and print is at risk, perhaps more than the bulkier terminals and personal computers used for online search. This has resulted in the investment of staff planning time and library dollars aimed at preventing theft, thus increasing the overhead costs of this particular format to the library.

OPTIMIZING THE FORMAT MIX

Obviously there is no one perfect format for reference material, nor is there one universal combination of formats which will answer the needs of all patrons everywhere, but what are the possibilities of determining the optimum mix for any given library? Once again, we can apply criteria which we already have in place for evaluating reference materials: how does each format rate when evaluated in terms of the goals of the institution, and the level of subject coverage desired? How is each format affected by staff availability: does the library have the staff available to perform online searches on demand, or to initiate patrons into the use of CD-ROM databases, or will some other method of providing information have to be used? Finally, and reluctantly, we have to be realistic enough to consider budget as well: can the library afford not just the subscriptions for optical disc sources, but the price of the equipment as well? The research done on queuing theory which has helped to determine the optimum number of terminals for online catalogs can be put to use in revised form to determine the number of workstations needed to make effective use of a given number of optical disc databases. Given the popularity of this technology in most libraries to date it is safe to predict a heavy future demand, but finding the funds to respond to that demand will be a challenge. Once again, history and tradition play a part: endowments, for instance, are an increasingly vital adjunct to the library's official budget, but they tend to be rigidly structured with extremely restrictive guidelines for use. A memorial terminal or CD-ROM drive lacks the emotional appeal of a book-plated special collection or a commemorative reading room, despite the fact that a fund offering annual payments is ideal for subscription purposes, including subscriptions to CD-ROM databases.

Staff availability is another all-important factor, as we mentioned above, and the library needs to have available comparisons of the time needed to help patrons with print sources, do online searches and teach the use of CD-ROM. Nor are these all the possible combinations; it is also feasible to have patrons doing their own online searches, or to have reference librarians doing CD-ROM searches by appointment for patrons. It is critically important that the library have a cohesive policy on how much the user is expected to do independently and how much the library staff will be available to help. Allocating a major portion of the reference budget to "self-service" sources such as CD-ROM indexes and full-text databases does not necessarily free up staff time, because any time which is liberated from doing online searching for patrons can easily be swallowed up in introducing and explaining the CD-ROM sources instead. Just as automation did not magically reduce the level of staffing required to run a quality library operation, so the introduction of optical information technology is not a panacea to solve all our reference problems. Automation allows us to offer superior service, however, and optical information systems enrich the choices available as we try to structure the reference area to be more responsive.

Other considerations for integrating the available formats into the reference collection include the advisability of trying full or partial cost recovery, and the impact of the new technology on the rest of the library.

It is tempting to try to retrieve some or all of the costs of optical disc or online database subscriptions by passing these costs on to the users. In a corporate library cost recovery is not an issue; the librarian has already won the battle once a budget including online or CD-ROM options has been approved. Cost containment, in the form of choosing the most efficient source compatible with the company's finances and information needs, is the problem here. In contrast, public and academic libraries frequently justify charging for online searches by saying that the patron is paying not for information, but for convenience: the same information is available in print form at a greater cost in time spent for retrieval. As more libraries switch over to new information technologies, the paper sources may no longer be available as backups; few libraries can justify continuing to subscribe to both CD-ROM and paper versions of the same information despite the relative savings offered by publishers for parallel subscriptions. Where does this leave the students, or members of the general public, who cannot afford information in high-tech format? We are on the way to inventing a new form of discrimination based on the ability to pay for method of delivery.

Another consideration is the effect of new information technology on the library outside the reference area. To give just one example, the dividing line between "reference" and "non-reference" becomes blurred when we look for the best location for CD-ROM periodical indexes. Should they be located in the reference area beside their print counterparts? In the periodicals area beside the titles they index, which would be appropriate in a totally "self-service" environment? In a different location with better security or better noise control for printers? Who controls access to the CD-ROM discs? Putting CD-ROM equipment with other reference tools may seem like the obvious choice, but is a busy reference desk really the best access point for equipment which may need intensive one-to-one instruction, may involve frequent trading of ID cards for discs, and deserves fairly steady oversight by a staff member? This is hardly the ideal scenario for the typical reference desk! In short, it is important not only to decide what to purchase and in what format, but to explore all the ramifications for the rest of the library before putting the new reference materials in place and declaring them a success.

In conclusion, it is impossible to structure the reference collection adequately without first knowing the goals of the library and the goals of the parent institution, and without determining the special needs of their clientele. Armed with this knowledge, the library can then decide how to respond to these needs, and because of the variety of formats in which many reference sources are now available, it is possible to set up the reference collection for service, or self-service, as is most appropriate. The equation for the ultimate format mix is an individual one which must be tailor-made to each reference area; even departmental collections in the same building may differ in their requirements, depending on their specific user profiles.

The most important point is that evaluation and maintenance of the reference area should be pro-active, not reactive: it should be the reference librarians who initiate and control the evolution of the collection to ensure needed continuity and flexibility, rather than fighting a rearguard action driven by external factors. We have more options available now than ever before to choose from in creating a reference collection which will be truly responsive to the needs of the institution and its clientele. It is our responsibility to see that we make the best and most intelligent use possible of these options in our various library settings.

NOTES

1. Sheila S. Intner and Jane Anne Hannigan. *The Library microcomputer environment: management issues*. Phoenix: Oryx Press, 1988, p. 89.

2. Nancy L. Eaton, Linda Brew MacDonald and Mara R. Saule. *CD-ROM and other optical information systems: implementation issues for libraries*. Phoenix: Oryx Press, 1989, p. 4.

Evaluation of Corporate Reference Collections

Daniel O. O'Connor
Esther R. Dyer

SUMMARY. Results of several research studies indicate that corporate reference collections may differ in kind and in definition from reference collections of other types of libraries. It was found that a corporate reference collection may not embody a "core"; it might not imply ownership of items; it might rely heavily on referral sources; and it might be redefined functionally as a window or gate to rentable information. The corporate librarian may make little distinction between a reference book and any other item in the library collection. Further, evaluation of such a corporate reference collection entails the evaluation of other parts of the library. This includes the ability of librarians to use any source to answer reference questions or provide information for the decision makers in the corporation; such a mode implies that the presence of a reference collection may be counterproductive to the provision of information services. Methods of evaluation were also considered as indicators of performance distinct from output measures.

DEFINITION AND EVALUATION
OF REFERENCE COLLECTIONS

The evaluation of corporate reference collections is plagued by an inherent contradiction: the collection contains materials relevant to prior corporate decisions and not to future ones. Therefore, it is

Daniel O. O'Connor is Associate Professor, Department of Library and Information Studies, Rutgers University, New Brunswick, NJ 08903. Esther R. Dyer is Director of Public Affairs, Empire Blue Cross and Blue Shield, 3 Park Avenue, New York, NY 10016.

not difficult but often irrelevant to evaluate "the reference collection." The corporate library supports the information needs of senior management; the library's collection exists to contribute to the corporation's next decision. As such, corporate library collections are unlike those found in public, academic or school libraries where repeated use of the same materials is a normal expectation. Corporate reference collections fulfill a purpose so special that their evaluation requires different assumptions and principles than those now available for other types of libraries.

Three major assumptions are inherent in current definitions of reference collections: (1) the reference collection is comprised of reference books; (2) the reference collection is designed for repeated use of its materials; and, (3) by analogy, the reference collection represents a "lock" with the reference question representing the "key." Further, it is *assumed* that these principles can be universally applied across *all* reference collections in all types of libraries.

Assumption 1: Reference Collection Contains Reference Books

The evaluation of a reference collection has traditionally been implied by discussing the characteristics of reference books. Katz treats evaluation of the reference collection in terms of its size, subject matter, and cost (Katz, 1987, pp. 208-212). In the reference evaluation literature there appears to be confusion between the evaluation of reference *service* and the reference *collection*. Most articles on evaluation of reference collections quickly move to the issues surrounding the evaluation of reference processes and services. It is suspected that this occurs because the assumptions surrounding reference collections are so ingrained in librarianship that their premises are not discussed. The root of this stems from the notion that reference collections are comprised of books which fit some particular definition; rarely are reference collections defined by the information needs of the library's users.

If the reference collection is simply the repository of reference books, then any set of reference books could constitute a core collection for any library. It is precisely this premise that would lead a library to assume that Sheehy (1986) embodies a core reference collection applicable to any library. Concomitantly, numerous articles extol the virtues of reference service with little attention as to how this relates to the reference collection. One possible exception to this is information and referral services (I & R) which are usually treated independent of a concrete reference collection (see the entire issue of *The Reference Librarian*, No. 21, edited by Middleton & Katz, 1988). Crowley describes the heart of an I & R service as a referral file of "agencies, organizations, and individuals with whom clients or patrons need to be linked" (Crowley, 1988, p. 22). The place of the traditional reference collection is not clear in I & R but what is paramount is the use of a specially compiled file to target a particular purpose.

Our analyses, however, of the reference activities at Empire Blue Cross and Blue Shield led to a distinction between those questions which relate to the strategic information needs of corporate decision makers and those questions which serve the educational and personal needs of staff. It was determined that the traditional reference collection was largely unneeded to serve corporate decision making. What was needed were specialized reports and directories, extensive statistical and technical information, selected government documents, and online access to bibliographic and full text databases.

Often questions could only be answered by using an information broker, such as FIND SVP, which was kept on retainer. In some cases, corporate decisions were served by proprietary compendia and proprietary technical or market reports, housed within the Corporate Archives. Almost without exception, these items would not have been useful in a traditional, static reference collection. Two tools were crucial in answering the questions of decision-makers: (1) the computer for online access to published information, and (2) the telephone for checking, updating and even investigating uncaptured information. The latter questions could include esoteric biographical information and unpublished positions on issues of elected and appointed officials. By and large, the traditional reference collection was not as useful as other sources in meeting the sophisticated and highly specialized information needs of executives.

Assumption 2: Reference Collections Are Designed for Repeated Use

The core reference collection at Empire Blue Cross and Blue Shield, however, was useful in serving the educational and personal needs of corporate employees. Such reference collections, designed for repeated use as found in public, academic and school libraries, were helpful to employees enrolled in diverse programs of study: business, insurance, health care policy and undergraduate programs. Yet, those same "student/employees" had access to the academic libraries where they were enrolled in coursework. Employees also used the corporate library for personal reading and for questions normally asked of public libraries. Examples of personal questions included personal etiquette, gardening, hobbies and sports information. When the library answered such questions, it encouraged more "public library" questions. When a plan to focus the information needs of senior management was outlined, the corporation endorsed the policy. By targeting this audience the Corporate Library was able to gain recognition of its key role in the life of the corporation. In short, too much use had been made of the library for continuing education or for personal information and not enough focus was on decision-making. The use of the corporate library as a satellite academic library was not cost effective and it strained resources, staff, and limited space. Further, it created and perpetuated the cyclical problem of defining the mission of the library and isolating its objectives.

Assumption 3: Reference Collection is "Lock"; Question is "Key"

The third assumption, the "lock" and "key" metaphor, is used in biological explanations of virus bonding. It can be applied to the reference situation where the question (represented by a "key") fits a particular information source (represented by a "lock"). It seemed to us that this metaphor allowed for a better understanding of the traditional reference collection as a "given" distinct from reference services. The traditional reference collection is viewed as static, fixed and concrete in this metaphor since the books cannot be changed. The question, on the other hand, is dynamic but subject to manipulation and change. Thus, the librarian negotiates the question and forces the patron to change their malleable "key" until it fits one of the unalterable "locks." Question negotiation can then be viewed as a exercise which forces users to change their questions until they can be answered by the books on hand.

A different philosophical approach would be to treat the question as fixed and the reference source as changeable. This is a reversal of the usual approach in the reference situation. The testing of this third assumption has not been accomplished except in the refocusing of emphasis from the collection to the user.

REFERENCE COLLECTION OWNERSHIP AND SIZE

It is often assumed that a reference collection exists independent of the users or of the intended use of the library. This position is contrary to the corporate information environment at Empire Blue Cross and Blue Shield where the ownership of items is less important than access to information. To define a reference collection as irrelevant defies the conventional wisdom in our field and it was with caution that we broached this issue. Our reference texts tend not to address this assumption; instead, they assume the collection exists and then discuss its size. For example, Katz states that it is impossible to identify the optimum size of a reference collection but "one may arbitrarily say a collection of 3000 reference books is ideal and, then, via experience and over the years modify up or down depending on other factors" (Katz, 1987, vol 2, p. 210).

Katz also resorts to a pragmatic test: "If the majority of questions are answered, quickly and correctly, by the collection then it is the optimum size" (Katz, 1987, vol 2, p. 210). This rule failed at Empire Blue Cross and Blue Shield because it assumed too much: questions which are answered perpetuate similar questions, questions which are not answered are no longer asked. The presumption of having questions answered equated with a good reference collection is similar to saying that if users continue to come to the library then it must be a good library. Such an analysis ignores the non-user who stopped using the library because it did not "perform" for that particular individual. The continuing education reference transactions at Empire Blue Cross and Blue Shield were quite successful but that did not mean that this function enhanced or supported the library's primary role – that of providing for the information needs of decision-makers. Thus, methods of evaluation were based on Clark and Curran's (1989) distinction between indicators of library performance and output measures. Performance measures are specified by librarians as desirable objectives; output measures are indicators of user activities. Clark and Curran note that certain high levels of user activity, such as circulation, may not in fact be desirable.

WEEDING AND EVALUATION ACTIVITIES

When the library was re-focused to support decision-making in the corporation, a number of activities were initiated. First, a systematic review of the reference collection resulted in most items being discarded. The only remaining titles left in reference were a skeletal collection of compendia, directories, dictionaries, indexing and abstracting services, and a newspaper clippings file relating to the purposes of Empire Blue Cross and Blue Shield. Then, the small circulating collection was weeded using the same criteria. The criteria for weeding the reference and circulating collections were not based on prior use since there was a change in the purpose of the library. In fact, not allowing use as a criterion created problems in the item-by-item evaluation of the collection. Three questions were asked of each title in the reference and circulating collections: (1) Is it probable that this book would support a future decision in the corporation? (2) Does this book bear the imprint of a major publisher in relevant subject areas? (3) Is this book a unique or stable source of this information or would such information or its updates be available through other sources?

The first criterion – support of future decisions – led to identification of topics of continuing interest (health care costs, smoking, AIDS, etc.). The second criterion – major publishers' works – entailed extensive use of *Choice* and other standard guides. This also led to a complete evaluation of all standing orders which resulted in an evaluation of the appropriateness of the majority of items in each series. In turn, a complete title-by-title evaluation of the journal collection was also performed. Drastic changes were made to standing orders and to journal subscriptions based on evaluative studies. The third criterion — unique or stable source — became impossible to apply and it was dropped from the list of evaluative and weeding criteria.

Four subject areas were determined as relevant: (1) health insurance and employee benefits; (2) latest theories in business, management, and labor, with special focus on those emanating from certain universities; (3) health policy and services with special emphasis on cost studies and public or societal programs; and, (4) government affairs and demographic information, with primary targets to population, income, business indicators and related statistics of the 28 counties in New York State served by Empire Blue Cross and Blue Shield.

The new design of the corporate library was based on a series of research investigations conducted at Empire Blue Cross and Blue Shield. This work was heavily influenced by the conceptual models incorporated in the presentations and publications of five individuals: Penniman (Penniman & Hawkins, 1988), Matarazzo (1986), White (1980), Lancaster (1988), and Buckland (1988). Related research also influenced our considerations: general evaluation models (Dyer & O'Connor, 1983), weeding (Hulser, 1986), journal deselection (Segal, 1986), referral and brokering services (Dustin, 1988; Demo & McClure, 1988), statistical models (O'Connor, 1984), executive services (Marvin, 1988), and knowledge based systems of the future (Travis, 1989).

Penniman has made a substantial contribution in re-defining the special library and he has been instrumental in separating access to information from ownership of books and journals. His dynamic kiosk or information access station, demonstrated at the 1985 IFLA/ NCLIS Conference in Chicago, redefined the boundaries of reference collections by de-emphasizing the importance of responding to yesterday's questions. The Penniman model did not assume the repeated use of the same materials which was pervasive in the public, academic and school libraries. Its emphasis on responding to new questions which may require totally different sources was appropriate to the model being considered at Empire Blue Cross and Blue Shield. White (1980) found that the reasons given to initiate journal subscriptions are totally different from the reasons offered when subscriptions are considered for cancellation. When Matarazzo (1986) explored the basis for excellence in corporate libraries he identified methods to define the end-users and objectives of the library's services and collection. Buckland (1988) dealt with the overall assumptions of evaluation; these were then applied to the reference situation. Lancaster (1988) and Kantor (1981) provided the framework and reasoning behind actual measurement processes.

The arguments for the interplay of evaluation and the design of new services was then honed using three very different approaches. Wallace's (1983) *Performance Measures in Illinois Special Libraries* provides evidence that the usual input and output statistics do not allow for escaping from the assumptions of the traditional library. The work of D'Elia (1980) builds on the premise that use is a function of user characteristics; this was juxtaposed with the view contained in ALA's *Output Measures* (1987) which assume that use is a function of library characteristics. Mondshcein (1988) combined these person and situation components in his dissertation which explored how uses of corporate libraries and selective dissemination of information correlated with research users' productivity and citations received. It was the combined influence of all of these studies which led to the challenges made of the traditional model of corporate reference collections.

STAFF REACTIONS

As in any bureaucracy, change met with staff resistance. Prior to our research and the re-orientation of the library, it had no access to online databases. In effect, the library was viewed as a supplemental and non-essential support service within the corporation. As a result the library staff was rated on the salary scales at the clerical levels equivalent to secretaries to senior officers. While the re-focusing and upgrading of the library meant, in effect, an upgrading of library staff positions, this did not equate with ready acceptance of new priorities. Part of the resistance undoubtedly was a result of a need for the staff to learn new skills—especially online searching—and to look at reference users in a new fashion. Previously, the collection policy had been scattered requiring numerous copies of journals to be circulated and additions to the collection included for academic courses. The systematic collection development plan, however, required a high level of sophistication and attention to new reviewing media. Not unexpectedly, staff resistance resulted in turnover and the concomitant recruitment of appropriately trained new staff. Although continuing education courses, training seminars and even tutors were provided, the original staff was unable to re-focus their thinking away from a public library and book oriented mentality to a philosophy of access to information rather than ownership of materials.

IMPLICATIONS FOR CORPORATE LIBRARIES

The information environment in each corporation is unique and requires that information managers understand the needs of users. Regardless of budgetary limits, it is impossible for any corporate library to respond to all the information needs of all potential users. In targeting users, the corporate library, in effect, establishes a goal. For Empire Blue Cross and Blue Shield, the goal of serving the strategic information needs of senior management was paramount. The information needs of middle management, unless on assignment from key officers, became a secondary consideration. If reference staff had the time, the research information would be forthcoming. Whereas for senior officers, the response time was immediate or for more lengthy questions insofar as possible within 24 hours. For officers, messenger or overnight service and instant purchase of documents was used to enhance response time. A middle manager, on the other hand, might have to wait several days and be subject to normal mails and interlibrary loans before obtaining external information.

As a result of the re-ordering of library priorities, the level of staff was upgraded to professional status within the company, the budget increased and library usage by senior management grew. In the budgetary process, this vision of the library as an important resource and a "window" to a broad spectrum of information was a determining factor in the library maintaining or expanding its budget and receiving funding to continue and to enhance online services.

CONCLUSION

As a result of our investigations, the evaluative literature on reference collection and services, and practical experience, we believe that the reference collection of a corporate library does not embody a core collection, and in fact means access rather than ownership of materials. In our experience, decision-makers do not care about the source of information but rather are concerned with the immediacy of response and the currency of information. The non-circulating or reference collection is a targeted collection of statistical information, compilations, directories and annuals that can be used to enhance reference service. Each corporation will have to develop a reference collection policy that reflects its own goals. Within the parameters of the corporate environment and the available resources, reference service may be targeted to key users or decision-makers or provide universal service to all employees. It is our belief that given the competitiveness of most corporate cultures for limited budgets, the corporate library that proves its utility and is integrated into the decision-making loop has the best chance for surviving and even expanding its activities.

REFERENCES

Buckland, Michael K. *Library Services in Theory and Context*. 2nd ed. Oxford; New York: Pergamon Press, 1988.

Clark, Philip and Curran, Charles. "Implications of Tying State Aid to Performance Measures." Papers presented at New Jersey Library Association Annual Conference, Atlantic City, NJ, May 4, 1989.

Crowley, Terence. "Evaluating I & R in Smaller Public Libraries." *The Reference Librarian*, No. 21, pp. 15-29, 1988.

Demo, Teresa L. and McClure, Charles R. "Information and Referral in the Academic Library: Lessons in Attitude and Service from the Public Library." *The Reference Librarian*, No. 21, pp. 95-108, 1988.

D'Elia, George. "The Development and Testing of a Conceptual Model of Public Library User Behavior." *Library Quarterly* 50(4):410-430, October 1980.

Dustin, M.J. "The MINITEX Reference Service: Publicly Funded Information Broker." *The Reference Librarian*, No. 22, pp. 133-143, 1988.

Dyer, Esther R. and O'Connor, Daniel O. "A Proposed Methodology to Evaluate School Libraries." *Journal of Educational Media & Library Sciences* 20(2):119-135, Winter 1983.

Hulser, Richard P. "Weeding in a Corporate Library as Part of a Collection Management Program." *Science and Technology Libraries* 6(3):1-9, Spring 1986.

Kantor, Paul B. "Levels of Output Related to Cost of Operation of Scientific and Technical Libraries." *Library Research* 3:1-28, Spring 1981.

Katz, William A. *Introduction to Reference Work.* Vol. II: *Reference Services and Reference Processes.* 5th ed. New York: McGraw-Hill, 1987.

Lancaster, F.W. *If You Want to Evaluate Your Library . . .* Champaign, Illinois: University of Illinois (Graduate School of Library and Information Science), 1988.

Matarazzo, James M. "A Field Study Defines Corporate Library Excellence." *American Libraries* 17(8):588-592, September 1986.

Marvin, Stephen. "ExeLS: Executive Library Services." *The Reference Librarian,* No. 22, pp. 145-160, 1988.

Mondschein, Lawrence G. *R&D Productivity: Relationship to Selective Dissemination of Information (SDI) in the Corporate Environment.* Ph.D. Dissertation, Graduate Program in Communication, Information, and Library Studies, Rutgers University, 1988.

O'Connor, Daniel O. "Network Statistics: A Statistical Model for Data Analysis and Networks." *Resource Sharing and Information Networks* 1(3/4):75-82, Spring/Summer 1984.

Output Measures for Public Libraries; A Manual of Standardized Procedures. 2nd ed. by Nancy Van House, Mary Jo Lynch, Charles McClure, Douglas Zweizig, and Eleanor Jo Rodger. Chicago: American Library Association, 1987.

Penniman, W. David, and Hawkins, Donald T. "The Library Network at AT&T." *Science and Technology Libraries* 8(2):3-24, Winter 1987/88.

Segal, Judith A. "Journal Deselection: A Literature Review and an Application." *Science and Technology Libraries* 6(3):25-42, Spring 1986.

Sheehy, Eugene P. *Guide to Reference Books.* 10th ed. Chicago: American Library Association, 1986.

Travis, Irene. "Knowledge-Based Systems in Information Work: A View of the Future." *The Reference Librarian,* No. 23, pp. 41-60, 1989.

Wallace, Danny P. *Performance Measures in Illinois Special Libraries.* Springfield, Illinois: Illinois State Library (Statistical Report No. 8), 1983.

White, Herbert S. "Factors in the Decision by Individuals and Libraries to Place or Cancel Subscriptions to Scholarly and Research Journals." *Library Quarterly* 50(3):287-309, July 1980.

Applying the Fairfax Plan to Reference Collection Management: A Strategy

Jane G. Goodwin
M. Lydia Patrick
Julie Pringle

SUMMARY. To make collection development more effective and efficient, the Fairfax Plan was developed by the Fairfax County (VA) Public Library (FCPL). The traditional method of individual selection was no longer working due to significantly increased demands on the collection. The volume of information requests received and circulation statistics steadily rose; meanwhile, additional intensive demands were made on the Material Selection Office. The Office was reorganized and FCPL has begun to take advantage of mechanisms vendors use to speed identification and acquisition of available items. Scope statements and profiles of collection areas have been developed to aid library staff and vendors. The evaluation method to determine success of the Fairfax Plan for reference collections concludes the article.

Developing and maintaining a reference collection for a library system without a central or main facility presents major management challenges. In 1980, Fairfax County Public Library (FCPL) reorganized into a regional library system, adopting a configuration to assure equal access to information and library materials to all residents throughout the 400 square mile County. Fairfax County

Jane G. Goodwin is Coordinator, Evaluation and Information Development, Fairfax County Public Library, 11216 Waples Mill Road, Fairfax, VA 22030. M. Lydia Patrick, Assistant Coordinator, Evaluation and Information Development, and Julie Pringle, Coordinator, Collection Development and Management, are also at the Fairfax County Public Library.

33

has evolved from a suburban residential community into a jurisdiction of emerging urban centers. There is no single focal center for the County, and the continuation of a central or headquarters library would have been an inappropriate response to development patterns.

The regional system has a pyramid structure with each regional library having satellite community and minibranches centered in six population centers. Two additional regional libraries planned for newly expanding communities are currently in the design phase. The County has grown rapidly over the last two decades from a population of 469,000 in 1970 to a projected 800,000 in 1990.[1] As is often true of burgeoning growth areas, Fairfax County suffers from serious traffic congestion. Road construction and public transportation have not kept pace with expansion. Library users cannot be expected to move freely from one library location to another to satisfy information needs. To provide all patrons equal opportunity to use the Library's resources, FCPL operates under the concept of "regional parity." This concept eliminated specialized collection development in regional and community libraries. Committed to an even distribution of resources throughout the County, FCPL equally supports collection development in the six regional libraries. Differences in community interests and demographic characteristics are reflected in the regionals' popular materials collections.

Fairfax County residents are sophisticated information users. Many are employed by the information industry and businesses ancillary to the Federal Government. The median Fairfax County adult educational level is 16.2 years and the median household income is about $62,000. More than 127,000 students are enrolled in Fairfax County Public Schools. It is the nation's tenth largest school system, with a reputation for academic excellence. All these factors create a demanding library public that heavily uses its libraries. FCPL's twenty-two branches circulated 8.3 million items during FY1988 and responded to an estimated 1.9 million information questions. Using circulation as an evaluative criteria, FCPL is the busiest among southern public libraries.[2]

The annual Information Services Study (ISS) conducted by FCPL, based on *Output Measures for Public Libraries,*[3] produces an annual estimate of reference transactions by library with a system summary, a reference transaction per capita figure, and a qualitative measure called the Reference Completion Rate. As defined in the manual, the Reference Completion Rate is the "proportion of reference transactions successfully completed on the same day that the question is asked, in the judgment of the librarian."[4] The measure is the staff person's opinion of the users' immediate success in having their questions answered. FCPL's reference completion rate, shown below for the last five ISS, is high, indicating that according to staff, materials and expertise are nearly always available to respond immediately to a user's query.

REFERENCE COMPLETION RATE[5]

FY1983	FY1984	FY1985	FY1986	FY1987	FY1988
83%	79%	81%	88%	89%	90%

Other library systems serving comparable populations report reference completion rates ranging from 69-87%. FCPL would be included in the upper quartile among libraries reporting this measure.[6]

A cooperative reference accuracy study conducted by FCPL and neighboring library systems in 1984[7] determined that materials deficiencies were not the cause of incorrect responses to telephone reference queries. Low "scores" on individual transactions most often resulted from poor interviewing skills, particularly the failure to ask a closure question that confirmed whether or not the caller got the information desired.

From a "bell and whistle" included in an early Information Services Study, FCPL learned that staff consulted reference and circulating collections about equally when searching for answers to patrons' questions. The reference collection alone was used for only 42% of the questions asked; the circulating collection was used 42% of the time, and both collections were used 16% of the time.[8] Based on the results of this study, most community libraries interfiled their reference and nonfiction collections. In community libraries most staff are enthusiastic about interfiled collections that group together materials according to subject classifications without regard for reading level or format. Many staff have said that the stigma of using children's materials is reduced for users when separate juvenile nonfiction sections are eliminated; this is particularly true for young adults. The large buildings and collections in regional libraries make this kind of interfiling impractical.

OFFICE OF COLLECTION DEVELOPMENT
AND MANAGEMENT

With the steady increase in library use shown by both circulation and information services statistics, FCPL's Office of Materials Selection was concentrating attention on meeting the overwhelming demand for circulating material. The Office built opening day collections for three new regional libraries in a four year time span, while maintaining materials support for the rest of the System. In addition, during the same period and without additional staff, the Selection Office also assumed responsibility for selecting all non-print media. Therefore, reference collections received less attention than needed. Standing orders and continuations lists became the safety net for updating reference resources. The System overview for reference collections suffered. The evaluation of how well reference materials were meeting users' needs as appropriate to FCPL's defined levels of service for regional, community, and mini-libraries was also jeopardized. Balance in reference collections was not monitored as closely as desired.

By 1987, it was apparent that a review of FCPL's collection assumptions and subsequently a revised approach to collection management were necessary. The Office of Materials Selection was reorganized and renamed the Office of Collection Development and Management with one Coordinator supervising all subject and format specialists. This arrangement is fundamentally important because it ensures a System-wide approach to collection development while preserving specialities in children's, reference, adults', and media services.

FAIRFAX PLAN

The reorganization to Collection Development and Management was accompanied by a new approach to selecting material. The volume and variety of materials needed by FCPL made the old method of traditional item-by-item selection impossible. Increased speed in providing new materials to library users also became a priority. Vera Fessler, Associate Director for Technical Operations, created the "Fairfax Plan." Outlined in Figure 1, this plan provides a hierarchy of FCPL collection areas and formats by patron use patterns. It also provides guidance for resource allocation. It is a flexible plan that can be modified yearly to respond to changing System priorities and community demands. Current collection priorities are indicated by numbers printed after category labels shown on Figure 1.

Scope statements are being written for each part of the collection shown in the Fairfax Plan. The scope statements include the following information:

— goals for that part of the collection; how this materials category helps fulfill the library's mission to the community
— readership level; concerned with the intended audience, may include level of reading difficulty
— format; physical materials format that is acceptable for inclusion in the collection
— language; text language that is acceptable; most FCPL reference materials are in English
— access level; degree of bibliographic control necessary for item access — i.e., full bibliographic records are needed for reference materials
— distribution; definition of collection depth required for library types — i.e., regional, community, and mini-library depth of subject coverage
— selection parameters; concerned with imprint date, size, country of origin, and cost that may limit inclusion in the collection

These scope statements form selection guidelines for Collection Development staff. They also assist communication between Collection Development and public service staff by providing definitions and limits to collections in regional, community, and mini-libraries.

Before the Materials Selection reorganization, items were selected on an individual title basis in many nonfiction and reference

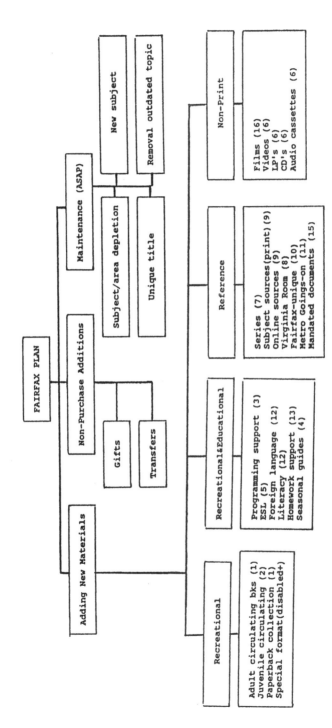

FIGURE 1. Fairfax Plan

areas. FCPL had not taken full advantage of the resources that major vendors could provide. Much of the preliminary assessment of the publishing market and projected titles, already done by many major vendors, was being duplicated by FCPL staff. The introduction of the Fairfax Plan shifted emphasis to subject coverage rather than specific title selection. Assistance was sought from two major vendors. One vendor works largely with bookstores and popular adult materials; the other works with materials for academic and research libraries. A two-step plan resulted for selection of materials in FCPL's adult circulating and reference collections.

POPULAR ADULT MATERIALS

Working closely with Ingram Library Services, Inc., FCPL experimented using the Ingram Advanced Buyer's Checklist (ABC) as a prepublication alert service. This was a response to the overwhelming dissatisfaction reported by branch staff at the tardy arrival of new current interest items, including bestsellers, under traditional post-publication selection plans. Before books are published, Ingram staff determine how many copies of a given title they will stock, based on their projections of its popularity. Ingram's customers using the ABC program, both libraries and bookstores, are encouraged to use a profiling system to project their own demand for these same titles and categories. A monthly list of reserved copies is produced for the client by Ingram. This list includes hardbacks, trade paperbacks, mass market paperbacks, and projected bestsellers. Numbers of copies can be changed and titles added or deleted by the customers. Unless notified of adjustments to the advanced shipping list, the items are shipped automatically by the vendor.

FCPL has used the Ingram ABC program for two years. It has been extremely time-saving and efficient as a way to get prompt notification and shipment for popular adult titles. ABC does not cover all publishers, nor does it relieve staff of maintaining awareness of titles covered in review media, books by local authors, or demand created by current events and cultural events. It does offer efficient and timely acquisition of the majority of new adult titles, thus freeing staff to focus on System-wide collection management and on more specialized areas of the collection. Some popular reference annuals are received as a part of the ABC plan. Assignment of new items to the circulating or reference collections is made by library staff when the item is cataloged. The vast majority of items acquired through the ABC plan become circulating material.

REFERENCE COLLECTION

Collection Development and Management will next devote attention to FCPL's reference collection. The overall goals of reference collection building are to develop and maintain concise reference collections that respond to users' needs for information and to provide for efficient acquisition of opening day reference collections for new libraries. The latter goal is particularly important to FCPL due to its aggressive capital improvement program.

The initial step in applying the Fairfax Plan to reference material is to develop scope statements for this collection category. The distribution portion of the scope statement, which defines varying levels of subject coverage for regionals, communities, and mini-libraries, will be the key to ensuring equal access to topical information for all users through the concept of regional parity.

The next task is to profile FCPL's desired reference collection using a subject thesaurus provided by the vendor to define collection levels further. Collection Development staff will do the preliminary profiling. They will then work with public service information specialists to fine-tune the levels of subject coverage expected. These activities will establish reference collection parameters for FCPL.

The process of developing scope statements and reference collection profiles will result in the following benefits to FCPL. Reference collection parameter definitions will help Collection Development staff work with vendors to notify FCPL of available, up-to-date materials that meet FCPL's needs. Utilizing vendor expertise to identify available titles, FCPL staff can devote more time and effort to other important areas of collection management. Additionally, these reference collection parameters will help identify areas of the existing collection that need attention and will guide in acquiring reference collections for new libraries.

EVALUATION PLAN

Reference collections should be responsive within System guidelines to users' needs for information. A special routine will be designed for an annual Information Services Study (ISS) to assess how well the reference collection plan defines materials needed to answer users' questions. Using general topics identified by Collection Development in the collection profile, staff will assign questions received during the survey period to a particular topic. The data collection sheet will be designed to record the question counts by these defined topics. After the tally sheets and procedures are pretested, information staff will log questions during a regular ISS. Using the data generated during the ISS, Collection Development will review the information and make changes, as appropriate, in the collection plan to supply the needed materials to respond to users' information requests.

After users' questions have been analyzed and adjustments have been made to the reference collection profile, individual branch reference collections will be examined based on collection parameters. Lists of branch holdings will be generated from the bibliographic database and item file with FCPL's new automated circulation system. Subject coverage for each branch will be assessed based on its holdings. Some titles may have to be individually examined to determine their "fit" within the overall scope outlined in the collection parameters.

Working with public information services staff, Collection Development staff will develop a core subject list of reference materials reflecting the depth of topic coverage outlined for each type of library. The core reference collection may be supplemented with other titles, as FCPL strives for regional parity in materials rather than exact duplication.

When existing reference materials have been reviewed, collection needs will be identified. Reference titles that do not fit the collection guidelines and titles that have been superseded by newer materials will be discarded. It may be necessary to prioritize subject areas within the collection that require refurbishing or supplementing. Immediate attention will be given to fill emergency needs, replacing lost materials and updating critical materials on a core list.

Collection Development staff will prepare a plan for a review cycle that will provide for ongoing reassessment of subject coverage for reference materials. The Collection Development staff will call on vendors to assist in collection profiling to identify titles that keep collections up to date. FCPL staff and vendors will become and continue to be partners in reference collection management.

REFERENCES

1. Fairfax County Office of Research and Statistics, *1988 Fairfax County Profile*. Fairfax County, Virginia, 1988.

2. "1989 Statistics of Southern Public Libraries," Memphis (TN) Public Library, unpublished.

3. Van House, Nancy A., and others, *Output Measures for Public Libraries*. Chicago: American Library Association, 1987.

4. Van House, p. 69.

5. Goodwin, Jane G., and M. Lydia Patrick, *Information Services Profile, Fairfax County Public Library, FY88*. Chicago: Public Library Association, 1988. p. 20.

6. Public Library Data Service, *Statistical Report '88*. Chicago: Public Library Association, 1988. P. 85.

7. Rodger, Eleanor Jo, *Reference Accuracy at the Fairfax County Public Library*. Chicago: Public Library Association, 1984.

8. Rodger, Eleanor Jo, and Jane G. Goodwin, *Information Services Profile: Fairfax County Public Library 1983*. Chicago: Public Library Association, 1983. p. 37.

Reference Collection Development Using the RLG Conspectus

Kathy E. Tezla

SUMMARY. Reference collection development should be seen as an integral part of the overall management of academic research library collections. The reference librarian benefits from participation in the development of collection development policy statements based on a collection evaluation using the Research Libraries Group (RLG) Conspectus. The writing of comprehensive collection development policy statements using the RLG Conspectus to evaluate subject collections requires that collection management librarians and reference librarians work closely together and integrate the development of the reference collection into overall collection development plans for the library. This article discusses some of the functions of collection management divisions and the potential components of a Conspectus-based comprehensive collection development policy statement. The sharing of the process between the collection management librarian and the reference librarian/selector is described. Benefits the reference librarian gains from the process are discussed.

Collection development decisions for academic research libraries involve considering not only the needs of the users who walk through the door today, but also the needs of future researchers. Unfortunately, this philosophy is not always applied to the academic research library's reference collection, which often becomes lost in the shuffle among collection management and public service responsibilities.[1]

Ideally, reference collection development should be seen as an

Kathy E. Tezla is Collection Management Librarian, Social Sciences Coordinator, and Reference Librarian at Woodruff General Library, Emory University, Atlanta, GA 30322.

43

integral part of the overall management of academic research library collections. Just as for the regular collections, decisions regarding the reference collections should be made within the context of the library's philosophy of service, taking into consideration the necessary tradeoffs between service to the user and the dictates of the library budget.

Such decisions require effective planning and coordination. Using the Research Libraries Group (RLG) Conspectus as the method for evaluation, public service and collection management librarians can work together to plan and create in-depth collection development policy statements that relate their library's reference to its general collections on a subject discipline basis.

COLLECTION MANAGEMENT DIVISIONS

To provide effective planning and coordination in collection development decisions, collection management divisions have been established within academic research libraries to spearhead collection development and evaluation programs. Formulating a collection management policy statement, conducting a collection analysis for the purpose of identifying strengths and weaknesses, overseeing the selection of materials, allocating and managing funds, addressing collection maintenance concerns (i.e., evaluation and replacement of lost materials and brittle books), reviewing gift collections, and interacting with library selectors, faculty, and students are a few of the principal functions performed by a collection management division in an academic library to facilitate its collection development and evaluation programs.[2]

However, collection management librarians find the formulation of a collection development policy statement to be the central and most integral part of their planning for the effective expenditure of the resources that have been allocated for the building of the library's collection during this era of accountability for service-oriented institutions.[3] Such a document reflects the incorporation of qualitative and quantitative criteria as a means to apply the library's objectives through its collection. A successful one should meet two overarching goals: (1) the standardization of data and its presentation, and (2) the provision of some means of measuring or estimating trends to support a budget request presented to the library and university administrations, a means of measurement which responds to demonstrated need and reflects both practical and philosophical concerns.

As an added benefit, the process of planning and creating a comprehensive collection development policy statement brings together collection management librarians who oversee the total holdings of the library and reference librarians/selectors, transforming the act of selection for the reference librarian from the simple addition of books to the library into a joint effort whereby attention is turned from individual titles to the entire collection, which is perceived as a whole. The collection development policy statement that emerges from this union can become the written foundation for effective decision making regarding both the allocation of the library's resources and the placement of titles in their appropriate locations within the library.

REFERENCE COLLECTION DEVELOPMENT

The way in which reference librarians/selectors interpret the role of the reference collection in the context of the library's general collection has a significant effect on their practices as developers of the collection. When selecting materials for the general collection, reference librarians with subject specialties constantly weigh the titles they select against some potential for reference use, whether they are reviewing weekly approval plan arrivals or ordering from publishers' catalogs. According to Kroll, in her article discussing the placement of reference collection development within the organizational structure of the library, reference librarians ask the following questions:

> Is the reference collection a microcosm of the entire library, mirroring its strengths and skipping lightly over the areas not represented in the general collection? Is the reference collection a narrowly focused set of tools dealing solely with the main interests of its primary users. . . . Or is it a broadly based set of information sources offering general knowledge in most areas with in-depth coverage of a select few? Or is it intended

as a place to go for the answer to any question in any field, regardless of the mission of the institution behind it?[4]

When reference librarians selecting materials for both the general and the reference collections answer these questions, they are defining both the nature of the reference collection and its function. No matter what service concept the reference department perceives itself to have, the development of its collection should be conducted within the context of the library's holdings, not as if it were a separate entity. When collection management divisions undertake the writing of comprehensive collection development policy statements, statements that incorporate the use of the Conspectus as the method for evaluating subject collections, collection management librarians and reference librarians must reach common understandings of the function of the reference collection, and work together to integrate its development into the overall collection development plans for the library.

THE CONSPECTUS

The Conspectus was first introduced in the 1970s as an inventory of academic research libraries' collections, as "the 'Conspectus' of collecting activity upon which cooperative endeavors might be built."[5] Over the years it has evolved into a comprehensive collection evaluation guide composed of several thousand subject subdivisions that can be used to reach a quantitative assessment of the depth of a library's current collecting, measured on a scale ranging from "0" (for "No Collection") to "5" (for the "Comprehensive" level) and with provision for recording goals for future collection building in different subject areas on the same scale. A language code, indicating the library's level of interest in collecting a mix of English and foreign-language material, is also assigned for each heading.[6]

Collection development policy statements are the final written product of a collection evaluation project. On one level they are clearly written declarations of the library's mission and goals for the management of its total collection within the context of and in support of the library's parent institution and users. On another level, when the findings of the evaluation are based on the Conspectus, the document becomes an assessment of collection activities in each specific subject area, which serves as a guide for the selecting of current and retrospective materials and the allocation of funds.

A collection development policy statement of this type would include the following components:

1. a *written narrative describing each subject field* in general terms, the courses taught (including changes and trends in course offerings) and the faculty (their areas of specialization and their research and publication activity, for the past five years and projections for the future), the number of undergraduates and graduate students enrolled in courses, the annual publishing activity in the subject field (for both monographs and journals), a description of the type of materials currently collected in the subject area and their estimated cost (monographs, journals, microfilm sets, foreign language materials), and a description of any coordinating or cooperative efforts (such as interdisciplinary programs with other departments on campus or with other academic institutions in the region or elsewhere).

2. a *numerical comparison of shelflist counts* in each subject area with those of selected institutions with similar programs.[7]

3. a *summary of strengths and weaknesses* of the collection in each subject area based on an analysis of the holdings of both books and journals, using checklists, standard lists, core collections, and the RLG Conspectus as guides.

SUBJECT PROFILE

Before undertaking the various steps involved in the creation of a subject-based collection development policy statement, it is first helpful to go through the process of defining the subject area, taking the time to outline the nature of the field and then describing the courses taught in the discipline, including a description of what the changes and trends in course offerings have been. This process can occur in a three-way consultation with the faculty (usually the faculty library representative for the academic department), the collection management librarian, and the reference librarian/selector. The definition of the subject field and how it is taught at one's own institution is needed to establish the appropriate context for the subsequent application of the Conspectus. The process of collecting this information combined with other components listed in (1) above helps to reveal the underlying global structure connecting collections and related academic programs, which should be reflected in the completed Conspectus.

SUBJECT AREA ANALYSIS

Working together, the collection management librarian and reference librarian/selector can examine the shelflist count. This examination involves taking each line of the Conspectus specifying classification numbers corresponding to a subject field and tabulating the number of titles to be found in the classifications, with statistics for average dates of publication and for languages represented. (Some libraries assign the gathering of this data to clerical support staff.) Using the guidelines provided, designated subject bibliographies are also checked against the holdings of the library to assess the percentage of monograph and serial titles held. This process forms the basis for judging the collection. It is one of the best ways of learning the depth and breadth of the collection, and the results should be reviewed before scanning the shelves.

Taking the data collected in the shelflist count and other Conspectus activities, the shelves of both the reference and the general collections are examined to determine the existing collection strength and current collecting intensity (i.e., level at which the library is currently buying in the area) for each line of the Conspectus.[8] The time that is required for this depends on the size and complexity of the subject field and the subject expertise of the selector. This phase of the process helps the reference librarian/selector and the collection management librarian to determine whether there are gaps in the holdings of either the reference or the general collection that require attention, and to raise the overall collection coverage to the particular optimum level of titles available.

FACULTY INTERVIEW

Some libraries have established a third category in their in-house version of the Conspectus, added to the existing collection strength (ECS) and current collecting intensity (CCI). This is the desired collecting intensity (DCI), and it indicates goals for future collection development in terms of the same codes used for the other two. Because the Conspectus is a collection based tool for evaluation, it is important to incorporate the library's clients into the evaluation process. This incorporation can be accomplished by a faculty survey or direct interviews with the faculty, after the evaluations of the existing collection strength and current collecting intensity (ECS and CCI) have been completed.[9] This affords the collection management librarian and reference librarian/selector an excellent opportunity to discuss the present state of the collection (ECS) and level of support (CCI) with the teaching faculty, and determine what the desired collecting intensity (DCI) is from the faculty's perspective. The benefits are increased communication, interaction, and cooperation between librarians and the teaching faculty.

CONCLUSION

Once avoided and now increasingly encouraged, collection development policy statements are emerging as significant management tools in academic research libraries. More library planning is emphasizing codification in the area of collection development. Increasingly, the RLG Conspectus is being selected as a tool for collection evaluation.

Once completed, the collection development policy statement provides a written record of past, current, and future collecting intensities that can serve as a helpful public service tool. It can be placed at the reference desk so that the reference librarian/selector can better respond to the "why" questions regarding such matters as the unavailability of a title, the size of the periodicals collection in a subject field, the lack of books on a particular subject, or the level of materials (basic or research) the library collects in a field.

The reference librarian benefits from participating in the creation of a Conspectus-based collection evaluation and policy statement.

Benefits include: (1) a better understanding of the nature of the reference collection and how it relates to other collections in related subjects and areas (e.g., special collections, microforms, government documents, collections on interdisciplinary subjects); (2) more information on the scope and depth of the collection in specific subject fields; (3) a clearer understanding of how a subject field is taught at the institution, which helps determine the use of basic and advanced reference tools; and (4) better collection development skills (e.g., measurement of patterns of library acquisition against publishing trends). The result is a more confident reference librarian, better equipped with specific data on the library's collections and more readily able to articulate the library's collection development functions.

REFERENCES

1. David G. Null. "Robbing Peter . . . Balancing Collection Development and Reference Responsibilities," *College & Research Libraries*, v. 49, no. 5 (September 1988), pp. 387-399.

2. For a concise presentation of collection management functions and organization models for collection management, see: James A. Cogswell. "The Organization of Collection Management Functions in Academic Research Libraries," *Journal of Academic Librarianship*, v. 13, no. 5 (November 1987), pp. 268-279. See also: Carol W. Cubberley. "Organization for Collection Development in Medium-Sized Academic Libraries," *Library Acquisitions: Practice & Theory*, v. 11, no. 4 (1987), pp. 297-323.

3. Bonita Bryant. "Collection Development Policies in Medium-Sized Academic Libraries," *Collection Building*, v. 2, no. 3 (1980), pp. 6-26.

4. Rebecca Kroll. "The Place of Reference Collection Development in the Organizational Structure of the Library," *RQ*, v. 25, no. 1 (Fall 1985), p. 98.

5. Anthony W. Ferguson, Joan Gant, & Joel S. Rutstein. "The RLG Conspectus: Its Uses and Benefits," *College & Research Libraries*, v. 49, no. 3 (May 1988), p. 198. Another excellent historical overview can be found in Nancy E. Gwinn & Paul Mosher. "Coordinating Collection Development: The RLG Conspectus," *College & Research Libraries*, v. 44, no. 2 (March 1983), pp. 128-144.

6. For a discussion of the Conspectus process, see: Larry R. Oberg. "Evaluating the Conspectus Approach for Smaller Library Collections," *College & Research Libraries*, v. 49, no. 3 (May 1988), pp. 187-196.

7. *Titles Classified by the Library of Congress Classification: National Shelflist Count. 1985*. Chicago: Resources & Technical Services Division, American Library Association, 1986.

8. Oberg, p. 193.
9. Bob Greene (Science Coordinator, Emory University) and Kathy E. Tezla (Social Sciences Coordinator, Emory University) developed two types of questionnaires they used with their faculty. See: Association of Research Libraries. Systems and Procedures Exchange Center. *Qualitative Collection Analysis: The Conspectus Methodology*. Edited by Deborah Jakubs. Spec Kit #151. (Washington, D.C.: Office of Management Studies, Association of Research Libraries, 1989), pp. 45-48.

II. MAKING POLICY DECISIONS

Weeding and Evaluating the Reference Collection: A Study of Policies and Practices in Academic and Public Libraries

Carol Truett

SUMMARY. This study examined the reference collection weeding and evaluation practices of a selected group of academic, public, and county library systems. Results revealed that only two of the fourteen libraries had written guidelines specifically for reference, and only one of these was a complete document. The most common unwritten criteria for weeding related to age and use of materials, and most libraries conducted systematic evaluation of the reference collection, primarily by means of comparisons to checklists or standard lists of recommended titles. However, most libraries did not regularly conduct formal use studies. The use of CD-ROM reference tools, which was fairly widespread and well accepted, was expected to have an increasingly significant impact on reference collection development in the future. Major findings are summarized, and a list of questions provided for further study and research.

Weeding has never been a popular activity for the average librarian. Sankowski (1987, p. 272) confirms this, stating that few librar-

Carol Truett is currently Adjunct Faculty member at Purdue University Calumet in Hammond, IN. She was formerly Associate Professor in the School of Library and Information Studies at the University of Hawaii in Honolulu. Her current address is: 192 E. 900 North, Chesterton, IN 46304.

ians are eager to jump into its implementation, probably a master-piece of understatement. He cites four reasons (from Gardner, 1981, p. 212) for this lack of enthusiasm: (1) accrediting agencies have led us to believe that bigger is better when it comes to library holdings; (2) weeding is costly, especially in professional time; (3) lack of the necessary time makes weeding a low priority; and (4) weeding is not easy.

While weeding of the reference collection in particular is not a topic widely discussed in the literature, at least two major studies in the 1980s focussed on reference collection maintenance, including weeding and evaluation. Biggs and Biggs (1987) surveyed reference collection development in academic libraries in 1985. Some of their major findings were: (1) a substantial number of libraries had no written policies to guide either reference selection or weeding; (2) use of the reference collection was believed to be low, yet most collections seemed unmanageably large and use studies were rarely done; and (3) the online availability of sources was viewed as increasingly important in reference acquisition and cancellation decisions.

A study conducted by Engeldinger (1986) in 1982 drew similar conclusions. This survey, also of academic libraries, found that of 377 respondents, 88% had no written policy, though over 81% claimed to have weeding practices of some sort. Frequency of use of reference materials was a major determinant for weeding for only 54% of the respondents, despite the fact that anticipated use was presumably a major consideration for selection. Use, when a factor in weeding, was generally "determined by the subjective judgments of the reference staff and their ability to remember. Only twenty-three libraries had conducted a use survey of their collection" (Engeldinger, 1986, p. 371). Engeldinger concluded that weeding appears to receive very low priority, and that there is relatively little formal attention given to the role of weeding in the management of the reference collection.

FOCUS OF THIS STUDY

The original focus of this study was simply weeding practices in academic reference departments. It rather quickly became apparent that weeding and evaluation were difficult, if not impossible, to separate either in actual practice or as processes to study. It was also decided public libraries should be included. No recent study has compared the weeding and evaluation practices of academic and public reference librarians; thus such a study could possibly provide new insights.

Because the researcher wished to use interviews as the primary data gathering method, rather than to duplicate the large-scale mail surveys used in the two previous studies cited, only a small group of libraries could be included. The decision was made to conduct in-depth exploratory interviews at a small number of libraries, in the hope of generating some useful hypotheses that could be tested in a followup study on a larger sampling at a later date. Thus the author has tried to be extremely cautious in generalizing from findings, instead focussing on the observation of trends and the formulation of questions to be asked in future studies.

THE STUDY SAMPLE

Fourteen libraries were included in the study. Nine were university libraries, including five libraries of main campus or autonomous universities (four public, one private), and four libraries of regional campuses of large state universities. The remaining five were public libraries (two city and three county library systems). All the libraries but one were located in the same region of the Midwest; the remaining library was an academic library in the Far West. For some main campuses where reference librarians were not available for interviews, the author used a mail survey duplicating the interview questions. All these librarians responded with "interviews" at least as informative as the personal interviews. Not a single librarian contacted for an interview refused. Average interviews lasted an hour to an hour and a half.

The university libraries ranged in size from 70,000 to over four million volumes, and the public systems from 85,000 to over 345,000 volumes. Only two university librarians did *not* know the size of the reference collection; the others gave exact figures or estimates ranging from 5,000 titles to 40,000 volumes. Surprisingly, no public librarians knew their reference collection size. Two estimated theirs to be 2,000 and 2,100 volumes, respectively; one mentioned a $39,000 reference budget; one blamed the lack of a figure on an old, incomplete shelflist.

All seemed much more certain of the size of the total library budget and the constituency they served. A county library system reported a $4.5 million budget. Two more public and four academic libraries reported budgets over one million which might have exceeded $4.5 million, since precise figures were not requested. Two public libraries and four university libraries fell in the $500,000-$1,000,000 range. No public library fell below $500,000, but two academic libraries did.

Professional staff varied from as few as three to as many as 95. Reference librarians ranged from a low of two to a high of 25. The smallest academic library student head count was 3,000, and the largest almost 34,000. Public library service area populations ranged from a little over 15,000 to 200,000, and registered borrowers from 12,507 to 167,787. All but one public library had 50% or more of eligible borrowers registered, and two had over 80%. (All stressed that this was a very current figure, with patrons required to reregister in the past two or three years, often because circulation had been automated.)

WRITTEN REFERENCE COLLECTION WEEDING/EVALUATION POLICIES

Twelve (86%) of the libraries reported no specific written policy to guide them in working with their reference collections; this percentage is almost exactly that found in Engeldinger's study. Only two libraries, both academic, reported written guidelines, one a six-page document just revised (in April 1989) and one a policy "in part" that turned out to be some written notes that could provide a draft for a later policy. Another academic librarian said she was going to write such a policy "some day." A fourth academic librarian reported that "an ad-hoc committee was appointed several years ago to put together a policy, but it never reached a final format or [was] approved."

Two public librarians stated that parts of their general materials selection policy referred to discarding and provided the pertinent sections. "Current usefulness" was the major criterion given in one, with state and local history and literary classics mentioned as exceptions. The other policy listed six general criteria and included guidelines such as dated material with little or no permanent value, misleading or factually inaccurate material, or material superseded by a new edition or a better title.

Only two libraries claimed to have no *unwritten* guidelines for weeding and evaluating the reference collection. One was the library that had just revised its written guidelines. The other was a library stating reference was covered in a detailed general collection development policy which it did not share with the author. Unwritten criteria given by libraries (with number of libraries mentioning them) included: age, currency, timeliness (9); use (7); newer edition available (6); suitability for circulating collection (3); historical significance (2); availability of newer or better title (1); budget constraints (1); standing order dispositions (older editions sent to branches) (1); appropriateness for collection (1); incomplete sets (1); judgments based on subject area expertise (1); and current listings in standard tools (e.g., Sheehy, *BIP*) (1).

The two primary considerations in weeding appear to be age (in which one might include "newer edition," "better title available," and "not found in current standard tools") and use. The author found little or no evidence that formal use studies were being conducted. However, several librarians mentioned methods of studying use, including placing hash marks in reference books consulted, counting or listing reference books placed on book trucks for reshelving, and informal discussions among staff. No library appeared to keep a detailed running list of reference books consulted in desk work.

The only library that specifically mentioned space as a major consideration for weeding was a university library that recently moved into new quarters, doubling available space. Lack of space had been a prime motivator in weeding previously. Even in the new facilities, however, reference collection space is limited, and the reference librarian's philosophy is that the reference collection changes, but it does not grow.

One public library claimed a tight budget caused selection "pre-weeding" by "cutting back on annual [publications] to every second or third year." An academic librarian weeded by comparing her library's holdings to the most current editions listed in Sheehy, *Books in Print*, *Books for College Libraries*, and *ARBA*, also weeding "if something else has replaced [a source] and is held in more critical acclaim."

BASIS FOR DESIGNATION AS A REFERENCE BOOK

Librarians were also asked "upon what basis is a book (or other relevant material) designated as reference?" The factors mentioned in responses (with number of libraries reporting them) included: type of tool or format (7); "obvious" or "standard" reference source (7); nature of expected use (brief consultation, heavy demand) (6); cataloger or other recommendation after purchase (4); strengths or weaknesses of existing collection (3); currency or importance of topic (3); security of material (2); cost (2); sources providing keys to others (indexes, etc.) (2); language (1); geographical area (1); chronological subject-area limitations (1); current size of collection (1); faculty request (1); questions currently unanswered (1); space considerations (1); importance to curriculum (1); subject related to institution (1); and uncataloged material (vertical file, etc.) (1).

It is obvious that despite the lack of written guidelines relating to the reference collection, reference librarians had little doubt about what was or was not a reference work, and the decision was usually made when the work was ordered. Heavy reliance was placed on a work's being reviewed or traditionally designated as a reference source, or being of a type almost always considered reference (e.g., dictionaries, encyclopedias). One respondent described this as a self-perpetuating cycle, which would be especially true for serials received as standing orders.

On the other hand, a major point made was that the decision to put something in reference was often highly personal and subjective. It was common for catalogers to suggest to reference librarians that something be considered for reference that was not ordered as such. Thus, a checkpoint was provided when books were received, important when one realizes that many were ordered without firsthand examination. Probably the most common situation mentioned was that material ordered by faculty or other librarian selectors was (because of price, format, or other features) deemed to have reference value and thus placed in that collection. At some of the universities (particularly branch campuses with small library staffs) nearly all material requested by faculty may be ordered with little or no review, or academic departments and library committee members may have great discretionary power in selection. A number of reference librarians mentioned a "new book" location or book truck as a final checkpoint where a reference designation may be made.

A couple of librarians mentioned the Z collection (in particular subject bibliographies) as a special problem in making reference decisions. The rule of thumb used by one was that general bibliographies went into reference, and highly specialized subject bibliographies into the circulating collection. Besides limiting collection size, it was felt this facilitates browsing by the general public, who are more likely to find a bibliography shelved with its subject. The often highly personal nature of reference designations was stressed even by librarians who had their processing done hundreds of miles away at the university's main campus.

The frequency of reconsidering policies for reference designation or selection was not addressed by most respondents. The few responses offered ranged from "almost never" to "every two years or more frequently, if needed." The latter statement was taken from a written policy that also stated that "items themselves are reevaluated as needed or as requested."

The question of *who* decides what becomes reference material is inextricably linked to the whole process of reference selection. The head of reference (in ten libraries) or the reference librarians (in four), either collectively or as individuals, almost universally made these decisions. However, several respondents stressed the heavy reliance placed upon group decision making. One academic librarian commented that while the head of reference made final decisions, this often involved "input from [the] Reference Collection Development Committee [consisting of the] head plus three reference librarians." Another academic librarian said that the head of reference decided but this was flexible, and academic department heads could also designate materials as reference.

REFERENCE COLLECTION
ADDITIONS AND WITHDRAWALS

Librarians were asked to provide a recent figure for the number of additions to and withdrawals from their reference collection. The most startling result was that only three (21%) of the libraries could tell exactly how many additions had been made to the reference collection in the most recent year, and only *one* library could provide an exact figure for withdrawals! Some comments made were: (1) additions vary from year to year and "the current goal is to maintain or, if possible, reduce overall size of the reference collection"; (2) weeding is an ongoing process and the library discarded "at least a [book] truckload"; (3) "almost none [are weeded] — put into regular [circulating] collection"; (4) approximately same number weeded as added; and (5) weeding for new editions only, little actually removed. Only public libraries could provide exact figures for either weeding or additions. One public and four academic libraries, or 36% of the sample, could not even estimate additions, nor could six academic and three public libraries (64% of the sample) cite figures for withdrawals. The figures given varied so widely as to defy categorization. Three public libraries reported additions of 129, of 571, and of 12,697 volumes (all exact figures), and one estimated "about a dozen new volumes" added in the past year, and about 100 the year before that. Only one public library could estimate withdrawals (50 titles). Two academic libraries estimated additions of 150 and of 250 titles, and three estimated added volumes (135, 200, and 1,000). The three academic libraries willing to estimate withdrawals gave figures of 250 titles, 10 to 15 volumes, and 600 volumes. It appears that additions greatly exceeded withdrawals, but so few exact figures were available that it is difficult to be certain.

While the small number of cases requires caution in interpretation, it is noteworthy that the majority of libraries did not keep track of withdrawals. There are many possible explanations for this. One possibility is that libraries may seldom totally withdraw reference materials, instead relocating them elsewhere. Weeded materials may go to branch collections or be put in storage. One county system had institutionalized this entire process. The head of reference mentioned annually going through all reference titles received on standing orders, deciding the disposition of items replaced by newer materials. Thus it had become a matter of standard procedure to relocate or dispose of such items, some going to circulation, others to branches. There was evidence that other county library systems followed this practice, particularly those with limited budgets. A kind of "hand me down" to the stepchildren (i.e., branches) system was used to stretch scarce financial resources.

The continuous nature of much reference collection weeding possibly makes it difficult to keep track of withdrawals, as does the complex nature of dispositions of "retired" editions or titles. Keeping track of these dispositions may be too complicated to be considered worthy of a library's time. But this does not entirely explain the lack of figures for reference collection additions, or the inability to provide total reference collection figures, which should be part of a library's inventory control. The fact that many reference materials are serials and part of a library's standing orders may be partially responsible, but certainly does not explain the lack entirely.

RESPONSIBILITY FOR AND FREQUENCY OF WEEDING

Responsibility for weeding in academic libraries appeared to be evenly distributed: in five libraries the department head did most or all of the task (in one case assisted by a clerk or professional), and in five libraries the reference staff weed in areas of subject specialization. The results might more strongly favor staff participation were a larger sample queried, but this is speculation on the author's part. In public libraries, weeding was a responsibility of reference heads: of the five public libraries, the head of reference was responsible in four (in two cases with a clerical or professional assistant), and reference librarians weeded in their subject specialties in only one. This was possibly a reflection of the smaller size of public libraries in general, but not of smaller reference staffs, since four academic library reference staffs were no larger than that of the smallest public library.

There appeared to be a tendency toward continuous or year round weeding of the reference collection: five academic libraries and three public libraries reported this. Also, many libraries followed a dual practice. One academic reference librarian reported "year round weeding with more work done during semester breaks," and another that "reference librarians weed on an informal, unstructured basis and as part of a special assignment, usually in a subject area." A public librarian stated that books were weeded every month, but large-scale weeding had been done two years previously. Libraries apparently adjusted this activity to coincide with seasonal fluctuations in workload—e.g., academic librarians had more free time between semesters.

MECHANICS OF THE WEEDING PROCESS

There appear to be no general descriptions of the actual mechanics of weeding, despite the many librarians who have shared "how we did it in Valley View Library" stories. The present study sought to determine precisely how libraries conducted their weeding. The overall impression was one of a highly labor intensive and tedious process. Seven libraries mentioned going through the reference collection shelf by shelf and book by book. Another four checked both shelflist and shelves concurrently, and only one seemed to weed primarily by use of the shelflist. One academic librarian went into considerable detail. Their clerk first checked the shelf list against the shelves. Book carts were used, and colored slips offering three options: retain and update, put in circulating collection, or discard. Preliminary decisions were reviewed by the head librarian or others, order cards made from the slips, and appropriate actions taken.

Academic librarians frequently mentioned that input from academic departments or faculty library committees was sought, particularly *after* preliminary weeding decisions were made, but *before* materials were permanently removed from reference, and, as one head librarian put it, they generally erred on the side of keeping things when in doubt. Other consultants used in weeding were the Head of Collection Development and outside librarians (Music, Maps, Special Collections) or subject specialists (such as those from the university's main campus). And while the head reference librarian was generally the final arbiter, many libraries stressed that weeding decisions were frequently based on group consensus and were participatory in nature. It was mentioned on several occasions that a source used infrequently by one librarian might be a favored source for another, and the resulting discourse was felt to be a valuable, albeit subjective, part of the weeding process.

RELATIONSHIP BETWEEN WEEDING AND EVALUATION

Respondents were asked about the relationship between weeding and evaluation and about procedures for evaluating their reference collections. An overwhelming majority (seven of nine academic and all five public libraries) used formal or systematic procedures to evaluate their reference collections. Librarians were asked how they perceived the relationship between weeding and evaluation, what the difference was in their libraries, and whether or not their libraries made a distinction. The responses showed a consensus — e.g., "same thing," "simultaneous," "one and the same process." The following comment illustrates how the relationship may extend to selection as well: "Weeding and evaluation is one process. . . . As we weed, we also check to see if new editions are available and what we lack in order to meet the service needs." This cyclical relationship was described by numerous respondents, one of whom stated weeding is seen in terms of deselection, getting rid of the out-of-date, and evaluation more in terms of selection. Another librarian was more precise:

> Weeding is a subset of evaluation. Evaluation involves broad areas of collections as well as individual titles. . . . We use standard guides and lists to evaluate our holdings in subject areas. Evaluation includes repair, replacement, acquisition as well as weeding. Weeding is strictly removal of items.

Procedures used to evaluate the reference collection most frequently included the use of checklists of standard or recommended titles, reported by eleven libraries (seven academic and four public). No other method was mentioned more than once, with the exception of using subject specialists (reported by two academic libraries). Academic libraries also reported considering percentages of materials in different parts of the collection (1) or support of university programs (1), and using informal evaluation, grouped by subject (1). Additional public library considerations were unanswered reference questions (1), use by patrons and librarians (1), and percentage of reference budget spent on parts of the collection (1). A number of librarians stressed that while evaluation was a necessary component of weeding, it was perhaps even more vital in selection. One public librarian was not sure formal evaluation was necessary, claiming that "the collection works for us."

Despite the prevalence of using checklists for evaluation, many were skeptical of this process, claiming unique academic curricula or clientele. Corresponding wide-ranging collections made reliance on standard lists difficult, if not of questionable value, in evaluation. Checklists used were as likely to be general in nature as they were to be specific reference book lists. Titles mentioned as used in evaluation included the *Public Library Catalog*, recommended reference book lists from *Library Journal*, *Best Reference Books*, *Booklist*, Sheehy's *Guide to Reference Books*, *Books for College Libraries*, *ARBA*, and even the most current edition of *Books in Print*.

EFFECT OF CD-ROMS ON REFERENCE COLLECTIONS

The final question asked of librarians was what effect, if any, they saw CD-ROM sources having on the reference collection and on the use of indexing tools. Eleven libraries had CD-ROM workstations, including all but one academic library. Of the three public libraries to have CD-ROM, only one made it available to the public, but the other two were about to do so.

Numerous titles were available. The three most popular were ERIC (both Silver Platter and Dialog versions), InfoTrac's Academic Index, and Standard & Poor's Compustat financial database. Other titles mentioned were PsycLit, the GPO Monthly Catalog, *Social Sciences Index, Reader's Guide*, Books in Print with Reviews Plus, Bookshelf, Facts on File News Digest, MEDLINE, and Compact Disclosure. One library claimed to have five CD-ROM databases, but did not specify which ones.

Librarians did not view CD-ROM as a panacea to all their reference problems. One commented "It won't really displace anything," and another that it is "better suited to small bits of information." One felt strongly that literary criticism should not be available on CD-ROM. However, the majority spoke very positively about the effects of CD-ROM and cited a number of additional titles as already targeted for future purchase. One library wanted to add CD-ROM databases for nursing and mathematics, another intended to replace hardcover chemistry and physics abstracts with MEDLINE, and a public library was replacing its copy of *Reader's Guide* in reference (but not in periodicals) by the use of CD-ROM.

In evaluating effects on the use of manual indexes and the rest of the reference collection, one librarian stated:

> with five CD-ROM databases duplicating print indexes, use of the print sources has noticeably declined. We have not, however, cancelled any subscriptions to the print sources. Computerized searching has increased interlibrary loan requests dramatically. We are still examining the effects and implications on collections and services.

Another predicted that "CD-ROM . . . will have a significant impact on the development of our reference collection in the future. Many indexing and multivolume reference publications will be replaced . . . simply because the search software makes . . . retrieval of information [easier]."

A few librarians expressed concern that students used *only* CD-ROM, which they themselves considered a supplemental means of research, and they felt it was replacing use of the manual *Reader's Guide*. Another agreed CD-ROM was simply "another tool," not a replacement for abstracts, though perhaps for indexes. There was general agreement that manual tools and CD-ROMs will both be needed, and general acceptance of CD-ROM as a valuable new reference format. CD-ROMs were described as "costly but essential new tools" and as needed to "help us handle our workload," but not as likely to lessen the reference librarian's workload. The increase in interlibrary loan requests has already been mentioned, and one public librarian reported a large increase (over 10,000) in the number of periodicals requested at the serials desk in her library, an increase attributed largely to CD-ROM searching. Another public librarian was concerned about not having the magazines requested, suggesting CD-ROMs will create new problems and service expectations for libraries.

CONCLUSIONS AND QUESTIONS
FOR FURTHER RESEARCH

While one must be cautious in making overly broad generalizations, the following conclusions are offered as a summary of this study's findings:

1. The weeding and evaluation of reference collections appears to be more an art than a science at this point.
2. Reference department size largely determines who does the weeding. Staffs large enough to use subject specialists in selection use them for evaluation and weeding, regardless of library type. With staffs of two to four, the head of reference or sometimes the library director does evaluation and weeding.
3. Budget and space considerations, thought to play a major role in weeding, do not seem as important to librarians themselves. Also, libraries add more items to reference than they withdraw, and collections are thus approaching, or have already reached, unwieldy sizes.
4. Virtually all reference librarians respect the importance of weeding; though lacking written guidelines, they often weed their collections continuously and can list a large number of unwritten weeding criteria. However, more formal use studies of reference sources could provide a more objective basis for weeding. Better inventory control procedures are also in order, especially given the lack of precise figures for collection growth or size.
5. The library providing the greatest volume of service (with three reference librarians on duty at all times) has begun to

formalize weeding and evaluation by establishing written guidelines for disposition of all reference standing order replacements. Were others to follow suit, increased inventory control could result.

6. Those who do not weed usually cite extenuating circumstances such as a lack of a budget for new materials or a small volume of reference queries for which the existing collection is adequate.

7. Reference librarians generally agree on selection criteria for reference (usually based on type and use of material), and most acquisitions processes provide checkpoints to consider items for reference that were not ordered as such.

8. The effect of CD-ROM products on services will increase as their number grows, and requires further study.

9. While weeding can be codified, it includes elements of subjectivity and requires professional judgement and experience. When rules are developed, professionals must establish them, revise and interpret them, and supervise their implementation. Checklists and recommended percentages are not as useful in weeding and evaluation as they are in selection.

10. Finally, weeding reference, like budgeting, is a dynamic, cyclical and continuous process. Selection, evaluation and weeding cannot be separated or viewed in isolation.

It is recommended that the following questions be explored in future research: Do written guidelines for weeding and evaluation result in smaller reference collections? Do smaller collections provide more efficient service to patrons? Does the absence of written guidelines indicate a neglect of weeding and evaluation? (This author thinks not.) If there is no measurable increase in service, can we justify the time and effort needed for written guidelines? Last but not least, how do CD-ROM products affect reference services and collections? In summary, we need more comparative studies of libraries with and without written reference collection development policies to determine their effect on reference performance. So few libraries have written policies at present that it is difficult to determine what form they should take and to what degree their benefits outweigh the effort of writing and implementing them.

REFERENCES

Biggs, M. and Biggs, V. "Reference Collection Development in Academic Libraries: Report of a Survey." *RQ* 27 (Fall 1987): 67-79.

Engeldinger, E. A. "Weeding of Academic Library Reference Collections: A Survey of Current Practice." *RQ* 25 (Spring 1986): 366-71.

Gardner, R. K. *Library Collections, Their Origin, Selection, and Development.* New York: McGraw-Hill, 1981.

Sankowski, A. "The Challenges in Developing Academic Library Collections." *Catholic Library World* 58 (May/June 1987): 269-72.

Scheduled Reference Collection Maintenance: The Rhode Island Experience

Elizabeth Futas
Jonathan S. Tryon

SUMMARY. In early 1989 a questionaire was sent to forty-eight public and twelve academic libraries in Rhode Island to ascertain the use of and attitudes toward schedules for reference collection maintenance. The great majority of libraries favored this approach to collection maintenance and most used such an approach, although the individual schedules varied greatly. Over seventy-five percent of the reporting libraries had or were in the process of developing written collection development policies, but few had any written policies concerning scheduled replacement and none had a written policy encompassing all the material replaced automatically on a schedule.

INTRODUCTION

A well-selected, up-to-date reference collection is the *sine qua non* of effective reference service. In order to maintain such a collection one must weed out old materials and replace them with new ones. A great percentage of reference materials are serials or at least are treated as serials by librarians when it comes to their selection, ordering and maintenance. When one considers that there are innumerable titles that are published annually or at least very frequently, one is readily aware that it would take reference librarians endless hours to review all updates individually and to make replacement selections. Thus a basic question arises: how do librarians cope with

Elizabeth Futas is Director and Jonathan S. Tryon is Associate Professor of the Graduate School of Library and Information Studies, University of Rhode Island, Rodman Hall, Kingston, RI 02881-0815.

the enormous task of maintaining their collections? And more specifically, do reference libraraians employ a written or at least locally understood collection development/replacement schedule? To determine this, Rhode Island public and academic libraries have been surveyed as a case study of a well-defined group. The survey was designed to determine the extent to which libraries utilized scheduled reference collection maintenance, to determine various considerations involved in this approach, and to determine whether a pattern could be found in the intervals at which certain reference works were replaced.

On its face, such a survey might seem an effort to elucidate the obvious. It is a given that libraries do use schedules to replace reference works, whether the arrangement is consciously thought out or merely the result of title by title decisions for standing orders over a period of time. The result of such decisions can have a profound effect on the quality of reference service that the reference staff can offer, and poor decisions can also result in a great waste of money due to the acceptance of unnecessary duplication or ordering of replacements that have been inadequately or unnecessarily revised. These questions are important but before they can be addressed it is necessary to determine the degree to which libraries utilize schedules for reference collection replacement. It is to this end that this survey is directed.

PREVIOUS RESEARCH

A search of the literature reveals little research directly dealing with the use of schedules for reference collection maintenance. Bailey, in the report of a 1983 survey of seventy-five small academic libraries, raises the question of scheduled replacement of encyclopedias.[1] There is, he notes, "an apparently widely accepted rule-of-thumb that new editions of encyclopedias should be purchased at least every five years."[2] He goes on to say, "One seeks in vain, however, for any justification of this rule or, for that matter, any indication of the extent to which it is presently followed."[3]

Biggs and Biggs, in their generally excellent report of a survey of reference collection development in 565 academic libraries, include a section on automatic selection of materials on the basis of category of material.[4] They found that nearly half the college libraries did not select automatically by category and that larger, more comprehensive libraries were even less likely to use this method of selection. No other research directly relevant to the present issue has been uncovered in the literature.

GUIDELINES

While a body of research on the subject of scheduled reference collection maintenance is lacking, there are a number of articles providing inspiration and guidance in maintaining up-to-date reference collections. Often their advice is in connection with weeding the reference collection, which is natural since the serial nature of much reference material means that the decision to weed and the decision to replace is in fact the same decision. Engeldinger's article on weeding in academic libraries mentions, in passing, the connection between the appearance of a new edition and the weeding of the old.[5] In 1982 Rettig presented a cautionary editorial on the dangers of allowing out-dated material to remain in the reference collection.[6] Gail Schlacter has recently followed up on this with a blueprint of what the Reference and Adult Services Division of ALA might do to foster the rationalization of reference collection upkeep.[7]

There is also a considerable body of concrete advice available in numerous articles dealing with weeding, much of which librarians faced with the task of actually developing a schedule for replacement of reference materials would find useful. Such articles often give only the sketchiest of reasons justifying the replacement decisions, but they are written by professionals or experts in the subject area and do provide a useful starting point to the process. Recent articles useful along these lines include those of Margaret Thrasher,[8] Margaret Irby Nichols[9] and Lynn Westbrook.[10] The "Reference Serials" column currently edited by Joan Berman that appears in *Reference Services Review* occasionally has material touching on the question of scheduled reference material replacement. Finally, an important discussion of the problem of over-supplementation and unnecessary duplication in collections was ably presented in a pair of articles by Kendall Svengalis.[11]

STATEMENT OF THE PROBLEM

Since maintenance of reference collections is considered by all to be an important part of the development of a collection, how do libraries deal with the replacement of reference materials in their collections? Are there written, oral, or traditional policies or methods for replacing older editions of such reference standbys as encyclopedias, dictionaries, manuals, and handbooks? In these days of ever increasing numbers of directories, do libraries always replace these and other annuals on a yearly basis? What information goes into the decision on the scheduling of replacements?

METHODOLOGY

There are advantages to the fact that Rhode Island's library community is small and compact. With forty-eight (48) public libraries and twelve (12) academic institutions comprising the entire population, it becomes relatively easy to find out how the State of Rhode Island's libraries deal with the problem of updating their reference collections. This is considered a case study because of the small number involved. For Rhode Island, however, it is the population. Others replicating this study may have to use sampling techniques unnecessary with such a small population. A three-page questionnaire was developed and sent out to the sixty libraries in the state in early February and March of 1989. By the deadline, thirty-two public libraries (66.7%) and eleven academic libraries (91.7%) had returned completed questionnaires. The return rate on the survey, therefore, was 71.7%, or forty-three returned.

As the libraries represented in this survey range from large (materials budgets over one million dollars) to very small (materials budgets under five thousand dollars), the range of answers probably represents a good cross section of all the libraries in the country of these two types. The reference collections represented range from very small (under 250 volumes) to very large (over 30,000 volumes). Of the forty-three participants in the survey, thirty-two (74.4%) had written policies for either materials selection or collection development, with three of these libraries' policies in preparation at the time of the survey. Revision of the policies was not consistent, with some never revised and four revised only last year. The reviewing aspect of the policy was even more variable, with many not ever reviewed and some reviewed on two to five year schedules.

QUESTIONS AND ANSWERS

A large number (67.4%) of those libraries returning the questionnaires did have established schedules for replacing major reference sets such as encyclopedias. This replacement schedule varied from yearly to every ten years to on a rotating basis, and the rotating basis tied with the five year term as the most popular answer. When the questions dealt with annuals, only nine libraries replaced them every year, while nineteen libraries sometimes replaced them every year, nine libraries replaced many every year and four libraries did not replace every year. While sets such as encyclopedias appear to be on a five year replacement or rotating schedule, annuals are not. Only one library replaced annuals on a five year schedule and the policies of the others varied, including every two years; two to three years; two, three or five years; and replacement dependent on two other factors of interest to the study: cost (2) and use (7).

The study asked questions about reasons for not replacing annuals. Among those who answered the question, the two areas of most concern were use (22 or 56.4%) and cost or budget for replacements (10 or 25.6%). Many libraries gave multiple reasons and in these cases only the first response was counted in the survey, although multiple reasons certainly can exist for not purchasing reference materials. Of great surprise was the low percentage that considered the rate at which material became out-dated as their primary factor in deciding not to purchase annually (.05%).

In the area of reference materials published frequently, although not annually, most libraries (26 or 63.4%) did not have a purchasing schedule for these types of materials. Schedules for those that did have them varied from two to three years to whenever a new edition is published, with most agreeing that it depended on the title. Again with this type of material, cost and use were the two most popular reasons for the decision to replace—not up-to-date material, demand, or condition (although those reasons did enter into decisions as secondary factors).

A large majority of libraries did not have a written schedule for replacement by category or by title (32 or 78.0%). Respondents were also asked questions about replacement schedules for specific popular reference titles and formats, and the chart in the Appendix summarizes policies for the replacement of individual reference titles in Rhode Island public and academic libraries.

In another section of the questionnaire, various questions soliciting subjective responses were asked, to round out the survey and to allow the respondents an opportunity to voice their opinions as professionals.

The first question asked was: "Do you think replacement by schedule of regularly published reference material is a sound policy?" It was answered overwhelmingly in the positive, although the question may have been worded in a way that produced such a response. Any qualifications of these responses were made mainly on the basis of budget and size, but many cautioned about the need for reviewing of schedules regularly. Considering how few review or revise their collection development policies, it would appear that, although generally favored, written policies for scheduled replacements might prove difficult to maintain. Of those who advocated scheduled replacement, standing orders were the most popular way to deal with their acquisition. Keeping in-house records was not a particularly close second method. Given the budget distribution of those answering the survey, their unwillingness to pay an outside agency (vendor, subscription agency, etc.) does not seem at all odd. Only five said they might consider it or would definitely do so and these represented the "richest" libraries.

ANALYSIS OF RETURNS

Although it is generally thought in Rhode Island that the scheduling of periodic acquisition of reference materials that come out at specific intervals is a good idea, the practice is not written into most collection development or materials selection policies. The reasons for this may be budgetary or cost factors or use of the item. Much of the purchasing of such materials is left in limbo as to the schedule on which they are bought. There is a professional consensus that better control over this material could be established if schedules were developed for specific formats or items. This is done only in the largest of libraries that have the money for automatic purchases, although it is the smallest of libraries that need the freedom of not having to order on an item by item basis.

CONCLUSIONS

Since the timing of revisions or reviews of written policy statements is not clearly articulated in many libraries, it is probably safer, if the scheduling of purchases of reference materials is to be done, to have a procedural document attached to the written collection development policy that states the scheduling of such acquisitions. In that way, revision of procedures can be done on an ad hoc basis without the strain on the governance structure of the library that is necessary for full revision of policy documents. Better procedures will insure consistency and help improve the quality of collections. A quality collection is what libraries strive for, and one way to achieve it is through a well-thought-out policy and procedures document.

REFERENCES

1. Edgar C. Bailey, Jr., "Acquisition and Use of General Encyclopedias in Small Academic Libraries," *RQ* 25:218-222 (Winter 1985).
2. *Ibid.*, p. 219.
3. *Ibid.*
4. Mary Biggs and Victor Biggs, "Reference Collection Development in Academic Libraries: Report of a Survey," *RQ* 27:67-79 (Fall 1987).
5. Eugene A. Engeldinger, "Weeding of Academic Library Reference Collections: A Survey of Current Practices," *RQ* 25:366-71 (Spring 1986).
6. James Rettig, "Love Canal in the Reference Stacks," *Reference Services Review* 10:7 (Winter 1982).
7. Gail Schlacter, "Obsolescence, Weeding, and Bibliographic Love Canals," *RQ* 28:7-8 (Fall 1988).
8. "Weeding and Replacement Ordering Utilizing On-Line Circulation Data and Community Subject Specialists," *U*N*A*B*A*S*H*E*D Librarian* 51:19-22 (1984) and 57:4-5 (1985).

9. "Weeding the Reference Collection," *Texas Library Journal* 62:204-6 (Winter 1986).

10. "Weeding Reference Serials," *The Serials Librarian* 10:81-100 (Summer 1986).

11. "Cost Effective Acquisitions: A State Law Library Perspective," *Law Librarians of New England News* 6:13, 16-20 (Dec. 1985) and "Cost Effective Acquisitions: A Follow-up," *Law Librarians of New England News* 7:11, 35-39 (May 1986).

APPENDIX: REPLACEMENT SCHEDULES

N/A	TITLES	ONE	TWO	3-5	NEW EDITIONS	OTHERS
17	American Library Dir.	9	6	2	5	4
3	Books in Print	21	4	2	9	4
19	Bowker Annual	12		2	8	2
6	Encyclopaedia Britanica	2	1	23		11
4	Encyclopedia Americana	1	2	28		8
8	Ency. of Associations	11	4	6	9	5
19	Gale Dir. of Pubs.	7	6	2	7	2
2	Guinness Bk. Wld. Records	19	7	5	6	4
26	Hdbk. Chem. & Physics	2	1	8	4	2
27	Municipal Yearbook	8	2	1	5	
5	PDR	15	5	4	9	5
2	Prov. Journal Almanac	30	1		10	
24	S&P Dir. of Corps.	10	1	1	7	
12	Statesman's Yearbook	15	2	2	8	4
9	Statistical Abstract US	18	4		10	2
4	Subject Guide BIP	14	5	7	7	6
10	Thomas' Register	10	4	6	5	8
16	Ulrich's Intl. Per. Dir.	10	3	5	5	4
17	Who's Who in America	10	2	5	7	2
1	World Almanac	30	1		11	
9	World Book Encyclopedia	3	5	20	1	5
	TYPES					
4	Atlases		5	9	14	11
8	Auto Repair Manuals	11	3	9	7	5
15	City Directories	10		2	12	4
3	Dictionaries, Abridged	1	2	12	10	15
2	Dictionaries, Unabridged			10	19	12
7	Etiquette Guides			1	11	15	9
7	Telephone Directories	20	4	1	9	2
8	Test Prep Manuals	4	2	11	11	7
8	Travel Books	5	9	9	6	6

CD-ROM Sources
in the Reference Collection:
Issues of Access and Maintenance

Mary Pagliero Popp
A. F. M. Fazle Kabir

SUMMARY. CD-ROM has become part of the library universe and increasing numbers of libraries are considering the acquisition of reference tools in the new format. Issues of evaluation and selection, hardware purchase, and budget are primary concerns in this decision. Many aspects of day-to-day maintenance and access to CD-ROM sources must also be considered in the evaluation process. These issues — space, security, the care and feeding of hardware and software, reference assistance, staffing and staff training, and user instruction — are vital to the success of CD-ROM in the library. Particular attention is focused on literature about training for staff and users.

CD-ROM (compact disk-read only memory) has moved into the library universe as a reference tool. Many libraries have embraced this new technology; others are still deciding about its appropriateness to their reference collections.

The new CD-ROM technology brings with it concerns about cost, selection criteria, and hardware purchase. These issues, while admittedly important and often exceedingly complex, are just the beginning. Libraries planning for CD-ROM or evaluating existing

---

Mary Pagliero Popp is Head, Library Instruction, Indiana University Libraries, Bloomington, IN 47405. A. F. M. Fazle Kabir is Assistant Professor, School of Library and Information Studies, Atlanta University, 223 James P. Brawley Dr., Atlanta, GA 30314.

77

compact disk installations must also pay attention to day-to-day maintenance and plan for effective patron access. This involves thinking about space, security, the care and feeding of hardware and software, reference assistance, staffing and staff training, and user instruction. None of these concerns is new to reference librarians. CD-ROM technology simply makes them more visible.

Planning insight for public service use of CD-ROM products can be gained by use of one of the many excellent checklists for CD-ROM selection. The most complete of these appear in the new book entitled *CD-ROM and Other Optical Information Systems: Implementation Issues for Libraries.*[1] Linda Stewart's "Picking CD-ROMs for Public Use" is a series of statements against which to compare products.[2] The RASD MARS checklist for end user searching is also very useful.[3] Practical responses to these questions will be described in this paper, based on the experiences of libraries using CD-ROM.

EQUIPMENT AND SOFTWARE SUPPORT

After the decision to incorporate a CD-ROM system is made, planning should be undertaken for equipment and software support, furniture, additional wiring, new electrical circuits, acquisition of high quality surge protectors, and for telephone lines for systems with online access (such as WILSONDISC). Extra computer boards may also be needed to make equipment function properly.

Libraries should budget for equipment repair, particularly as equipment ages. Supplies for printers (paper and ink) are a significant expense.

New disks and software releases must be installed with regularity. The advent of Local Area Networks (LANs) applied to CD-ROMs will require system reconfiguration and programming.

Eaton, MacDonald and Saule also point out that building maintenance and custodial staff should be involved in planning for cleaning the equipment and the area around it to minimize accidental damage.[4]

SPACE AND SECURITY

Space and security issues impact on one another and on staffing needs. There are two major models for space planning: development of a separate end-user searching facility or placement of computers in a public area within easy view of the reference desk. In either case, space must be set aside for patrons waiting to use equipment.

Texas A & M,[5] the University of Vermont,[6] and Oregon State University[7] have set up separate search centers containing both optical disk and online end-user products. These areas are staffed by student workers who check disks in and out, maintain the equipment, and provide basic user instruction, referring more complicated questions to the reference desk. Reese and Steffey[8] discuss the advantages and disadvantages of these plans.

Most libraries have placed their CD-ROM stations near the reference desk and use reference staff to support both the stations and the patrons. A telephone survey by Young and Miller found that 73% of their respondents had this model.[9] In such a setting plans must be made for security of the compact disks. (Eaton, MacDonald and Saule point out that most CD-ROM publishers do not replace lost or stolen disks for free.[10]) Some relevant questions should be tackled at this stage. Will the disks be checked out (as a reserve item)? Will use be restricted to certain groups? Will staff or patrons change the disks? Will the CD-ROM disk be available all hours the library is open or only when the reference desk is staffed? Young and Miller also found that more than 60% of their respondents made the disks available during all library hours and that 46% stored the disk in the disk drive. Barbara Timm Kosinsky writes that her library uses 3 CD-ROM products on one machine and allows patrons to change disks based on clear instructions posted at the stations with few problems.[11]

Other necessary security measures include use of locking disk drives, deleting all DOS files (especially FORMAT) from the hard disk, converting as many files as possible to read only, and backing up the hard disk[12] using a special program such as FASTBACK.

Libraries have experimented with use of sign up sheets or signs indicating time limits. Time limits and appointment times vary from 15 minutes for relatively easy-to-use databases to 2 hours for more complex sources. 30 minutes seems the most frequently used time period. Time limits must allow time for learning by inexperienced users. Reese and Steffey list the advantages and disadvantages of both methods and raise useful questions, such as, how far in advance to allow sign-up and what to do about latecomers.[13] Experience at Indiana University shows that users are not hesitant to ask for the station when it is their turn.

STAFF AND STAFF TRAINING

Eaton, MacDonald and Saule identify seven management and maintenance questions that must be asked in staff planning, covering such topics as oversight and coordinating responsibilities, communication with vendors, maintenance of equipment and supplies, assisting patrons, training searchers and preparing instructional materials, evaluation, and bibliographic control. They observe that any set-up will work well if it reflects the library's administrative structure and the strengths of the staff, emphasizing that coordination, maintenance and instructional responsibility must be assigned.[14] Number, level, cost and training of staff will be dependent upon the location model chosen — separate facility vs. reference area-based, and the type of user training offered.

Starr and Butcher provide a student monitor job description for staff in their separate facility.[15] These students are also assigned to design user handouts, signage, and keyboard templates.

Regardless of the staffing model chosen, all reference staff and all public services staff on duty when the reference desk is closed must have a clear understanding of their responsibilities toward the CD-ROM stations. They must also be given training to enable them to carry out those responsibilities.

Staff training is both an important and an expensive issue. Coons and Stewart state that they have "realized that everyone on the staff needs to learn more about CD-ROM than we previously thought."[16] Harter and Jackson observe that "staff training will be a significant issue in terms of time and money" because training sessions and practice time must be planned for each CD-ROM system.[17]

MacDonald suggests a useful training model. The trainer becomes completely familiar with the CD-ROM product, evaluates the staff's knowledge of hardware and of database principles, develops a systematic plan for training, including decisions about the amount of training each level of staff member needs, and prepares lessons and practice exercises.[18]

The issue of prior knowledge of staff is an important one and affects the length of learning time. Online searchers will already know database structure and Boolean logic. Others might have to learn to use a microcomputer as well as learn the database and its commands. To take these issues into account, Downing recommends allowing at least a month before a staff member is expected to assist patrons.[19]

Eaton, MacDonald and Saule assert that all public services staff who will work with optical disk databases be "specially trained in both technical aspects of microcomputer/CD-player management and database searching techniques." They should know the microcomputer keyboard and the operation of special keys (function or cursor) in the database, and how to change disks, to restart a system, and to trouble-shoot a minor problem, such as a paper jam. Staff should be taught database structure, Boolean logic and searching techniques for each optical system used, as well as the location of user aids, such as the thesaurus. Staff should also know how to request help from the appropriate sources.[20] Harter and Jackson add that reference librarians should be "aware of concepts of information storage and retrieval such as record and file structures, characteristics and limitations of controlled vocabularies and natural language, stop words and sorting rules" and be able to teach this information to users. Staff must also understand the need to stay informed of changes in the software.[21]

Staff practice time is essential, preferably *before* the system is put out for public use. In addition, clear manuals of policies and procedures are necessary (and must be continually updated). A good example of a procedures manual for staff is excerpted in an article by Kenneth Murr.[22] It was created for end-user searching at Clemson University, but, with modifications, could work well in an optical disk setting.

Hahnemann University library staff have developed an extensive training program for staff. As part of the program, they have devised a list of hardware and software skills required of the staff who assist new users. At Hahnemann, "full-time staff have participated in a hardware skills seminar. In addition, reference and circulation staff attend one-hour seminars for each database" followed by one-on-one review sessions.[23]

A final staffing issue is the need for a technical support person. CD-ROM systems and software are technically sophisticated. New software releases and new disks must be installed. Trouble-shooting of equipment problems and work with vendors must be done. Libraries have planned for technical support in a variety of ways. Texas A & M relies on computer science students to install software and computer boards, trouble-shoot the equipment, and write simple programs.[24] The Reference Department at Indiana University reconfigured an existing support staff position. The job responsibilities are described in a recent article in *The Electronic Library*.[25]

USER FRIENDLINESS

Many writers have delineated the characteristics of user-friendly CD-ROM databases. Duchesne and Giesbrecht define some of these characteristics as: availability of context-specific on-screen help, on-screen explanation of meanings of commands and menu items, browsing for search terms, and shortcut methods for experienced searchers.[26] Herther refers to "readability" and arrangement of information on screens, appropriate use of abbreviations, windows and graphics, logic in the commands and in the search process, and minimal numbers of keystrokes.[27]

Publishers of CD-ROM databases maintain that their products are so user-friendly that users need no training. However, as Starr and Butcher point out, "suppliers assume, when they write their software, that all users understand search strategy formulation and Boolean algebra."[28] Nicholl describes "irritating features" which include poor error handling, problems with menu options and difficulty moving between menus, and obscure commands.[29]

Tutorials and help screens might be useful, but many are too long and it is difficult to find exactly the information needed. Documentation can also be very helpful. However, few CD-ROM publishers provide the full range of materials users need, such as on-screen tutorials, brief searching guides, key templates and detailed manuals.

In light of these problems, some type of user instruction is necessary.

USER INSTRUCTION

Examine Your Assumptions and Goals

Harter and Jackson make a basic statement of belief based on their assumptions about user knowledge when they state:

> Transferring databases and search software from mainframe computers and magnetic disks to microcomputers and optical disks will not make instant experts out of end-users who have no knowledge or understanding of concepts and principles of information retrieval, even though some librarians and system promoters have taken this position.

Further, they believe that it is "essential to determine the minimum level of knowledge and skill . . . users . . . must have to satisfy their information needs using a given system."[30]

Librarians who believe in user education and in maximizing access to all users have also formed goals and objectives to support CD-ROM instructional efforts. These determine the instructional methods used by individual libraries. At Cornell's Mann Library staff have developed the following goals: CD-ROM sources are available to anyone, are to be treated similarly to the printed reference works they resemble, allow for a free self-service alternative to online sources, and "provide an opportunity to teach users about the organization and retrieval of information." Their reasons for teaching CD-ROM skills are: it is useful to teach CD-ROM skills to present the basic concepts in the information literacy curriculum and the context of other print and non-print resources; the products are "not self-explanatory;" and Cornell students must not be at a competitive disadvantage because they lack skills of information literacy and technology use.[31] Hahnemann University Library uses its CD-ROM instruction program to "promote CD-ROM usage, increase user effectiveness, and reduce the load of new user instruction on reference and circulation staff."[32]

Library Experiences of User Search Effectiveness

The Indiana University Libraries have had some form of optical disk source since 1985. In the intervening years, librarians have realized that patrons learn the mechanics of computer database use quickly, but often fail to grasp the underlying concepts of the search process and to transfer their learning from one source to another. Specifically, users have difficulty in choosing an appropriate database, in focusing topics into researchable questions, in recognizing and using controlled vocabularies, in analyzing the topic and conceptualizing the key concepts, and in combining those concepts in a way that the computer can process them (Boolean logic). Users also have difficulty in understanding that the computer may not contain everything ever written on the topic, in evaluating the sources they find, and in locating materials in the library.

Other libraries report similar experiences. For example, Karp found that advanced search procedures, such as truncation and Boolean logic, were little used among ABI/Inform searchers. Tooey and Raimondo found like problems among their PsycLIT users. Capodagli, Markidian and Uva found that Medline users overestimated the completeness of the disk in the machine, when they have in fact searched only one year of literature.[33]

The Research

Two recent research studies emphasize the need for instruction in database use. Linde and Bergstrom found that teaching the contents of a database increased user speed and reduced errors. Teaching of the theoretical structure of the database without teaching about the content led to some inadequate search schemes but subjects still learned to use the database more quickly than those given no training.[34] Stewart and Olsen found that students trained in logical operators and vocabulary control were more effective in using ERIC on CD-ROM.[35]

Nancy Herther summarized the findings of microcomputer training studies as they might affect CD-ROM use.[36] Class-like settings are preferred by many for training. User support should be passive but easily available when needed and is more important as the system becomes more complex. User support will build knowledge and make difficult tasks seem easy. It is more effective when given by a human. Support should be centered on the user's needs and it should provide a background frame of reference for understanding the system.

Training—A Prerequisite for Use

The University of Vermont requires that students using databases other than WILSONDISC and Dow Jones complete a workshop training session, a computer-assisted instruction (CAI) tutorial, or a workbook tutorial before using the equipment for the first time.[37] This approach has trained large numbers of users (1000 in 1987), but it is expensive and may not be for all libraries.

WHAT TO TEACH USERS

Based on the problems of users, instruction should include: how to identify the information needed; how to choose an appropriate source; contents, scope and limitations of the database under discussion; other related sources (to provide context); and basic search commands and techniques for the system at hand. Instruction should take into account the user's familiarity with computers and provide some extra help for those not yet computer literate. Instruction should also include how to locate materials in the library. Practice should be an integral part of formal training, but it must be relevant to the users. For example, the user may start with an assigned general topic and then go on to search his/her own topic with practice prompts.

Eaton, MacDonald and Saule suggest that instruction should address basic skills for use in any database. These are: database structure, formulation of a research topic, isolating main concepts, understanding basic Boolean operators, special search techniques (e.g., truncation), how to modify a search, and the use of print, display and download options.[38]

Since much CD-ROM instruction is done at the reference desk, the Hahnemann training protocol will be useful to consider. The protocol was developed to help library staff balance CD-ROM user instruction with other reference questions, providing enough information to get the user started. It includes description of the database and its coverage, important keyboard features, important display features and logical operators, basic search strategy, ways to combine terms, and user aids.[39]

INSTRUCTION IDEAS

Libraries have adopted varied methods of instruction in CD-ROM use.[40] Some are traditional in nature, such as widely advertised formal training seminars and walk-in instructional sessions, brief information sheets about each product, and integration of CD-ROM instruction into the regular program of user education. Materials are placed at the workstation in many libraries, including sample records, quick reference guide sheets or command summaries, posters, and flipcharts; keyboard templates or labeled function keys are often used. A few libraries have used search planning worksheets, self-instructional workbooks, tutorials on computer disk, or expert systems.

Three innovative approaches are worth special mention. Scripps Institution of Oceanography Library has a menu-driven library developed set of help screens on the hard disk of the computer where the CD-ROM version of *Aquatic Sciences and Fisheries Abstracts* is mounted.[41] Librarians at Texas A & M used computer presentation software to allow search screens to be captured and incorporated into a graphic instructional presentation with a script for use in training large classes to use InfoTrac.[42] A school librarian in Washington State teaches the concepts involved in database searching by having her students build their own computer database.[43]

Equipment for training is also important. Patrons really want hands-on computer training, which is not always possible. At Indiana University librarians give demonstrations using a computer, a CD-ROM unit and a computer projection unit.[44] These are moved to a separate classroom. Two potential problems arise from this plan—it takes a system away from patron use and requires movement of delicate computer equipment. Use of a portable computer with a graphics card and appropriate expansion slots would improve this situation.

Reality

Despite many efforts at CD-ROM user instruction, it seems likely that many users will resist such training unless they really need it. For example, a recent study showed that only 36% of a student user group felt that instruction by a librarian was needed to successfully use a CD-ROM source; in fact only 39% of the group asked for help.[45]

A realistic approach seems to be to develop many sources and levels of instruction, including brief instructions and command summaries at the CD-ROM workstation, handouts, formal instruction sessions devoted to an individual CD-ROM source, incorporation of CD-ROM sources into regular bibliographic instruction sessions, search worksheets/planning sheets, and clear easy-access online help materials. Much of the instruction for CD-ROM sources will continue to be done one-on-one at the reference desk and libraries may simply have to accept this fact as they plan for staffing and for the costs involved.

IMPACT ON LIBRARY SERVICES AND COLLECTIONS

The greatest impact seems to be the increased volume of business at the reference desk.[46] When InfoTrac was introduced into the Undergraduate Library at Indiana University, reference questions increased more than 100%, with patrons asking about equipment use, search strategies, and how to find needed periodical articles. An additional staff member had to be added to the desk staff at peak periods of each day. This level of use has remained high for more than 3 years.

Librarians believe that use of periodicals and microforms has also increased as a result of CD-ROM use. The literature does not reflect any consensus as yet about effects on online searches and interlibrary loan.

Libraries planning to add popular CD-ROM sources should also plan to handle increased business at the reference desk. In addition, librarians should be prepared to invest more time and effort in bibliographic instruction activities.

Publicity

The most effective publicity for CD-ROM sources is word of mouth. Most libraries who have written about their programs use standard publicity activities: signs, posters, flyers, and newspaper or newsletter articles to introduce new sources to prospective users. Incorporation of CD-ROM products into the regular bibliographic instruction sessions also spreads the word.

In a recent article, David Taylor asserts that academic libraries must actively publicize new CD-ROM services to make certain everyone who might benefit from the services learns about them and to gain political points with the university administration.[47] A good example of such a program is that of Texas A & M which includes news releases, paid advertisements, and special mailings to teaching departments.[48]

Planning — The Key to Success

Librarians should consider all relevant issues when incorporating CD-ROM sources into the reference collection. Factors, such as staff training and user instruction, which were not quite so compelling when libraries considered addition of traditional reference sources have now become very visible in the CD-ROM environment. The problems are not insurmountable and thorough planning will result in better reference service.

REFERENCES

1. Nancy L. Eaton, Linda Brew MacDonald, and Mara R. Saule, *CD-ROM and Other Optical Information Systems: Implementation Issues for Libraries* (Phoenix, AZ: Oryx Press, 1989), 69-72.

2. Linda Stewart, "Picking CD-ROMs for Public Use," *American Libraries* 18(October 1987) 738-740.

3. Direct Patron Access to Computer-based Reference Systems Committee, "Planning for End-User Searching: A Checklist of Questions," *RASD Update* 8(April-June 1987):14-16.

4. Eaton, MacDonald and Saule, p. 67.

5. Sandra L. Tucker et al., "How to Manage an Extensive Laserdisk Installation: The Texas A & M Experience," *Online* 12(May 1988):34-46.

6. Charles M. Peters, "Laser Disc-Based Services for End Users," in Martin Kesselman and Sarah B. Watstein, eds., *End-User Searching: Services and Providers* (Chicago: ALA, 1988), 192-193.

7. Karen J. Starr and Karyle S. Butcher, "Establishing a Compact Disk Reference Center at OSU: Some Considerations," *The Laserdisk Professional* 1(July 1988):82-89.

8. Jean Reese and Ramona J. Steffey, "The Seven Deadly Sins of CD-ROM," *The Laserdisk Professional* 1(July 1988):20-21.

9. Judith E. Young and Lewis R. Miller, "Integrating CD-ROM: Some Advice from the Field," *CD-ROM Librarian* 3(April 1988):11.

10. Eaton, MacDonald and Saule, p. 54.

11. Barbara Timm Kosinsky, "Three on One: Maximizing Patron Access to CD-ROMS," *The Laserdisk Professional* 1(November 1988):107.

12. Karen J. Starr, "Taming the CD-ROM Wilderness: Developing and Managing a Workstation," *The Laserdisk Professional* 1(November 1988):51-52.

13. Reese and Steffey, "The Seven Deadly Sins of CD-ROM," p. 22.

14. Eaton, MacDonald and Saule, pp. 52-53.

15. Starr and Butcher, p. 89.

16. Bill Coons and Linda Stewart, "Mainstreaming CD-ROM into Library Operations," *The Laserdisk Professional* 1(September 1988):40.

17. Stephen P. Harter and Susan M. Jackson, "Optical Disc Systems in Libraries: Problems and Issues," *RQ* 27(Summer 1988):520.

18. Linda Brew MacDonald, "Training Library Staff to Use CD-ROM," *Access Faxon* 1(Spring 1988):6-8.

19. Jeff Downing, "Planning for CD-ROM Technology: Or, How to Stop Worrying and Embrace the CD-ROM," *Reference Services Review* 16, no. 3(1988):26.

20. Eaton, MacDonald, and Saule, p. 63.

21. Harter and Jackson, p. 520.

22. Kenneth Murr, "The Clemson University Library Training Manual," *Small Computers in Libraries* 7(December 1987):40-44.

23. Howard Silver, "Managing a CDROM Installation . . . A Case Study at Hahnemann University," *Online* 12(March 1988):65, 62.

24. Tucker et al., p. 39.

25. Ann Bristow, "Reference Sources on CD-ROM at Indiana University," *The Electronic Library* 6(February 1988):26.

26. Roddy Duchesne and Walter W. Giesbrecht, "CD-ROM: An Introduction," *Canadian Library Journal* 45(August 1988):220.

27. Nancy Herther, "How to Evaluate Reference Materials on CD-ROM," *Online* 12(March 1988):107.

28. Starr and Butcher, p. 87.

29. Paul Travis Nicholls, "Laser/Optical Data Base Products: Evaluation and Selection," *Canadian Library Journal* 45(October 1988):298.

30. Harter and Jackson, p. 519-20.

31. Coons and Stewart, p. 33, 37.

32. Silver, p. 63.

33. Nancy S. Karp, "ABI/Inform on CD-ROM: A First Look," *The Laserdisk Professional* 1(May 1988):34. Mary Joan Tooey and Paula G. Raimondo, "CD-ROM: A New Technology for Libraries," *Medical Reference Services Quarterly* 6(Fall 1987):10. James A. Capodagli, Jackie Markidian, and Peter A. Uva, "MEDLINE on Compact Disc: End-User Searching on Compact Cambridge," *Bulletin of the Medical Library Association* 76(April 1988):182-183.

34. Lena Linde and Monica Bergstrom, "Impact of Prior Knowledge of Informational Content and Organization on Learning Search Principles in a Database," *Contemporary Educational Psychology* 13, no. 2(1988):90-101.

35. Linda Stewart and Jan Olsen, "Compact Disk Databases: Are They Good for Users?" Online 12(May 1988):52.

36. Nancy Herther, "Microcomputer Technology: Helping Users Cope," *Online* 12(September 1988):120-122.

37. Eaton, MacDonald, and Saule, p. 105.

38. Eaton, MacDonald. and Saule, p. 61. Two other useful sources of ideas are: RASD MARS Direct Patron Access to Computer-Based Reference Systems Committee, "Library Users and Online Systems: Suggested Objectives for Library Instruction," *RQ* 25(Winter 1985):195-197. ACRL BIS Task Force on Model Statement of Objectives, "Model Statement of Objectives for Academic Bibliographic Instruction: Draft Revision," *College and Research Libraries News* 48(May 1987):256-261 (particularly the section on "How information sources are intellectually accessed by users").

39. Silver, p. 62, 65.

40. For example: Coons and Stewart, pp. 35-37. Eaton, MacDonald and Saule, pp. 61-63, 105. Timothy Jewell, "CD-ROM and End-Users: The University of Washington Experience," *CD-ROM Librarian* 4(January 1989): 20. Alice Littlejohn and Joan M. Parker, "Compact Disks in an Academic Library: Developing an Evaluation Methodology," *The Laserdisk Professional* 1(May 1988):39. Reese & Steffey, "The Seven Deadly Sins of CD-ROM," p. 21. Tooey and Raimondo, pp. 9-12.

41. Two articles describe the programming software in some detail: Peter Brueggeman, "ASFA on CD-ROM at Scripps Institution," *The Laserdisk Professional* 1(July 1988):39-47. Peter Brueggeman, "Online Help for CD-ROM Database Searching," *CD-ROM Librarian* 3(May 1988):10-14.

42. Susan K. Charles, Keith A. Waddle, and Jacqueline B. Hambric, "Using Presentation Software to Train Laserdisk Database Users," *The Laserdisk Professional* 1(November 1988):91-95.

43. Joan Newman, "What Does the Information Age Mean to Us?" *TechTrends* 33(October 1988):50.

44. For more information about computer projection units, see Scott Davis and Marsha Miller, "New Projection Technology for Online Instruction," *Technicalities* 8(February 1988):3-9.

45. Kristine Salomon and Kim Schultz, "CD ROM Use in an Academic Library: A Study of End-User Responses," poster session presented at the ACRL Annual Conference, Cincinnati, Ohio, April 1989.

46. For example, Silver, p. 62; Eaton, MacDonald and Saule, p. 107; Young and Miller, p. 12.

47. David Taylor, "Reference ROMs: Six Implications for Libraries Building CD-ROM Database Services," *American Libraries* 20(May 1989):454.

48. Tucker et al., pp. 41-42.

Client-Driven Reference Collections for the 1990s

Marie B. Waters

SUMMARY. The experiences of the 1980s have shaped us for the next decade. Escalating serials costs, space constraints, budget cuts in materials and personnel have required us to examine closely whom we serve and clarify the mission of the library. Based upon these realities, with a firm idea of the support we have from users, we need to focus on communication and interaction with all who use the collection (including administrative groups), and continue to improve the structures for collection development, maintenance and weeding.

Reference librarians in the University Research Library at UCLA are poised for the 1990s, and indeed, for the year 2000. For almost the entire decade of the 1980s, space constraints within the Reference Department's Reading Room, because of the expansion of the reference collection to accommodate extensive runs of biographic sets, annuals, periodical indexes, and national bibliographies, have been an ongoing challenge. In 1986 UCLA began to experience severe declines in the materials budget, escalation in serial costs, and devaluation of the dollar, and we have been forced to make serious and painful examinations of what we buy. In recent years personnel cuts have affected our ability to provide reference assistance at a level consistent with the past. This article discusses how these factors have influenced our reference collection management organization, strategies, and decisions, and why I believe we are stronger for having survived. First I will describe reference collec-

Marie B. Waters is Head of the Collection Development Division of the Reference Department, University Research Library, UCLA, 405 Hilgard Avenue, Los Angeles, CA 90024.

93

tion development within the UCLA Library administrative environment and as a function of our Reference Department. I will detail how costs, space, and personnel shortages have contributed to making this a tough decade. The article then addresses our decision to closely identify whom we serve as the basis for collection management decisions. The article concludes with comments on the structures and mechanisms to facilitate communication now in place within the Reference Department to move us into the 1990s.

ADMINISTRATIVE ENVIRONMENT

The UCLA Library receives richly deserved admiration for its reference collections, housed in the Reference Department's Reading Room, University Research Library stacks, and in the Southern Regional Storage Facility. The Library administration, led by Russell Shank, University Librarian, fully appreciate the value of reference sources in a research environment. Dr. Shank has long articulated the philosophy that if UCLA cannot afford to buy all the books our users require, we will at least have the reference sources to identify what is available. Therefore, UCLA is rich in library catalogs, bibliographies, indexes, and other tools that access literature and collections other than our own. The Associate University Librarian for Public Services, Ruth Gibbs, endorses the Reference Department policy to serve our primary clientele — UCLA's faculty and students — in their programmatic and research missions. Karin Wittenborg, the Assistant University Librarian for Collection Development, is an active advocate for meeting these needs within budgetary limitations. She has created campus-wide organizational structures for fruitful collaboration among selectors to reduce unnecessary duplication of collections and to formulate collection policies to minimize overlapping. Through her internal structure great progress has been made in identifying and prioritizing collection management needs and in establishing guidelines and better lines of communication among selecting units.

It is now well established that the University Research Library Stacks and the Southern Regional Storage Facility are extensions of the reference collection. The Reference Department, frequently in collaboration with the Bibliographers who select for the University Research Library, sends many titles to these locations, where they may be designated Building Use or Non-Circulating. Catalogers and faculty are also consulted in determining best location of major reference materials. The selection and funding of reference sources are primarily the responsibility of the Reference Department, but Bibliographers often order titles which they offer for retention in the Reference Department. Occasionally a Bibliographer prefers the Library to have a circulating copy of a reference work or a copy housed in a special University Research Library unit, such as the Microform Service. In those cases the Reference Department is informed and does not take the title out of the processing pipeline. If we want a copy for our own Department, we purchase it out of Reference funds.

UCLA'S REFERENCE DEPARTMENT

The Reference Department of the University Research Library serves primarily the research and teaching needs of faculty and students in the social sciences and the humanities. Our reference collection includes the national bibliographies which serve all disciplines, and we are a central referral point to the other 18 libraries on campus. As a flagship reference department, providing professional reference assistance the longest number of hours of any campus library, we have a strong general reference collection.

Under the general direction of Ann Hinckley, Head of the Reference Department, our Collection Development Division, which I have headed since 1980, is responsible for planning, monitoring, and supervising the departmental book budget, and decides what books are selected for the reference collection and where in the Library they are housed. As public service librarians we also serve at the Reference Desk, and participate in other public service activities such as database searching and bibliographic lectures. As assigned by our Collection Development Division, all reference librarians participate in some aspect of collection management, such as evaluating a new book for the collection, analyzing reference collection strength within a discipline, serving on the departmental weeding committee, reviewing reference publishers' ads, or taking responsibility for the department's CD ROM collection.

TOUGH DECADE

As stated earlier, the 1980s have been a tough decade. Collection development librarians in the United States responsible for strong foreign language holdings will concur that the decline in the purchasing power of the dollar abroad has had a turbulent and negative impact on book budgets. UCLA has certainly been affected by this devaluation. Over 20% of the holdings in the Reference Department are in foreign languages, and our budget has been disastrously hurt. We fund the national and many of the trade bibliographies and collect major foreign encyclopedias, bibliographies, and catalogs. The University's strong emphasis on foreign languages, cultures, and programs requires correspondingly rich and extensive reference sources.

An additional piece of the budgetary equation is that reference collections are typically serial-dependent. At UCLA we spend at least 85% of our allocation on serial titles. Without careful monitoring, subscriptions could run away with the budget. During the 1980s, when even domestic continuations were experiencing price increases that outpaced inflation, we tagged several titles for evaluation when the invoices arrived. On a case-by-case basis we approved renewal. We also discovered by the mid-1980s that we were running out of space for these expanding serial titles. In less than 10 years the Reference Reading Room had grown from approximately 40,000 to over 47,000 volumes. We needed relief with the budget and with space.

RELIEF WITH THE BUDGET

To stay within budget, in the fiscal year 1986/87 we examined every one of our reference titles received as a subscription or a standing order. We cancelled many important tools we previously thought we could not live without. This examination has continued. In selecting monographic works for purchase we have been extremely judicious. We developed the following categories for cancellation and selection, which are currently in use:

- Popular titles. Titles which may be less scholarly or which are not needed in the direct support of the teaching and research programs will be cancelled. For example, *Magill's Masterplots*, *Something About the Author* and the *New York Times Biographical Service*, all popular, useful, and convenient resources, are not essential to our function, and we no longer have them in the Reference Department.
- Practical, how-to titles. Although consulted by staff and faculty, we discontinued *Phonefiche*. From experience we knew it was consulted primarily by off-campus patrons, and we needed the considerable savings cancellation would provide.
- Back-up subscriptions. We no longer have the luxury of second, back-up copies to the *Readers' Guide*, *Ulrich's*, and the *MLA Bibliography*. We will hold dog-eared, tattered, mended, rebound copies of these titles until replacement is the ONLY alternative. Users may have to wait their turn to use the single copy.
- Duplicate subscriptions in the same building. The ease of access to materials held in the same building makes this a high priority.
- Duplicate subscriptions on the same campus. UCLA has many special libraries which serve disciplines overlapping ours. We made selective cancellations of titles in subjects such as art, music, business, and education. The Music Library subscribes to the *Music Index*, and it was with considerable pain that we cancelled our subscription, as the index is a major source for articles on dance and theater, two academic departments we serve. We reason that patrons needing this resource will also benefit from the expertise of UCLA's music librarians and the more extensive reference collection the Music Library houses.
- Spin-off titles. Publishers such as ABC/CLIO issue many useful titles from their database files. When we already hold the information in one form (such as *America: History and Life*) we require a compelling reason to acquire a spin-off.
- Titles not essential for yearly purchase. If currency is not ab-

solutely essential, we rotate purchase, ordering every three or four years. Titles such as *Statistics Sources* and *International Acronyms, Initialisms, and Abbreviations Dictionary* fall into this category.
- Expensive titles. All titles over $200 are evaluated in consultation with other reference collection development librarians. We also confer with selectors outside the Reference Department, and we have been very successful in collaborative funding.

We saved the most money in serials cancellations. These savings amounted to 15% of our total materials budget. We also trimmed our volume count by transferring out of the Reading Room those titles we dropped. With a modest augmentation from the Library administration, this savings has allowed us to ride out increased serial costs and the effect of dollar devaluation without overspending our allocation.

How and with whom did we discuss these cancellations? As a policy, UCLA selectors send lists of proposed cancellations to all of the library units on campus for input before the final decision is made. The titles being considered for cancellation in the Reference Department were discussed with appropriate faculty, bibliographers, and selectors.

It is useful to have a record of our cuts. We prepared lists of titles we cancelled and of monographic works we could not afford to purchase. These lists have been used for documenting our restoration needs. They are also helpful in preparing purchase proposals when extramural funds become available. We continue to add to the lists and update them regularly.

SPACE

To reduce the size of the reference collection, in the mid-1980s we appointed a Weeding Committee of three reference librarians charged with the responsibility of meeting weekly to identify and recommend titles for transfer out of the Reference Reading Room. This committee was originally composed of the Assistant Head of the Collection Development Division (acting as chair), the Head of the Computer Reference Services section, and the Head of the Public Services Division. They reported to me. Over the years the composition of the committee has changed, and we try to find a diversity of viewpoints. This committee is responsible for recommendations for ongoing maintenance and for small crisis management of the collections within the Reference Reading Room. The committee now reports to the Assistant Head of the Collection Development Division, who is no longer a member of the committee.

However, in Fall 1988, several issues converged to focus special attention on reference collection management. We continued to experience the crunch in the materials budget, and we needed to explore, in a forum that would include all the reference librarians, the disciplines we would continue to serve. We wanted to discuss transferring some of the national bibliographies and back runs of biographic sets to the University Research Library Stacks. We needed to discuss the possibility for cancellation of printed tools superseded by our new CD ROM subscriptions. It was very clear that we could not purchase and house all the materials we wanted.

The Reference Department scheduled a series of two-hour "Weeding Forums" for all Department librarians. The convener of these Forums, who is also the Assistant Head of the Collection Development Division, solicited proposals in advance, and circulated these responses prior to our meetings. In each of these Forums, our reference librarians, all of whom are familiar with programmatic needs of our clientele, articulate collection needs and argue priorities. These meetings have allowed us to debate freely and air all issues. Differences are compromised or resolved democratically.

I have been delighted with the vigor brought to these discussions. As necessary, individual reference librarians consulted faculty and library staff regarding our concerns and reported back. With this added input we reached collection decisions regarding the best housing of national bibliographies, library catalogs, and back runs of biographic sets. With the concurrence of the bibliographers and the catalog librarians we directed many of these titles to the University Research Library Stacks, designated "Building Use Only." With the participation of the Head of Technical Processing in the Reference Department we were able to work out the procedures by which these transfers could be effected. These Weeding Forums have been an outstanding mechanism for reaching accord on major transfer decisions.

Another issue for the Weeding Forum has been the concern to make access to materials in the Reference Reading Room as logical and "user-friendly" as possible. Traditional clustering of abstracts, indexes, biographies, encyclopedias, catalogs, and other sources by type of tool in the Reading Room rather than by call number had made users dependent on the librarian for locating a desired title. Our Desk Collection, a non-public area, had also grown and patrons were waiting in line to request books.

Limited availability of funds for Reference Desk staffing does not allow us to use our time as circulation librarians. Formerly, our Reference Department staffed the busy hours of the Desk with three librarians. Present allocation allows for single or double staffing only.

We knew that with the easy access provided by ORION, the Library's online catalog, the patron would be able to query the computer for the item or subject desired and easily locate the call number if we could do away with the jumble of special shelving units. In one of the Weeding Forums we decided to do away with this confusion. By arranging the Reading Room in straight call number order the user will go directly to the appropriate place on the shelf. We also decided to dramatically reduce the Desk Collection, integrating most of it into the single call number scheme.

In this reference collection for the 1990s we agreed that there will be a "Librarian" collection of titles such as *Sheehy*, the *World Almanac*, *Ulrich's* and some other democratically selected tools that we need to do our work. The decisions about what "librarian" tools are needed in this small collection are stimulating questions about our philosophy of service. For instance, do we best serve our client by making him wait while we fetch a book or dig for the information, or is he better served by being shown how to access information? From our experience faculty and students prefer to have books and materials available for their use, on the shelves. Our public, being the University public, has the skill and ability to use ORION and a well-arranged collection. In effect, our collection development is client-driven in what we select and in how we make the collection accessible. Plans are now underway for this conversion.

STRUCTURES AND MECHANISMS
FOR COMMUNICATION

The Weeding Forums and the Weeding Committee have been two important structures for communication among reference librarians. We need to be informed as fully as possible about our collections. We also need ongoing clarification regarding whom we serve, the direction of new research, and how we organize the reference collection. We can use the Weeding structures to provide the opportunity to share and bring together librarians in the collection management process. There are other mechanisms for communication which have worked particularly well for management of the reference collection.

One of my responsibilities is to meet weekly with the Assistant University Librarian for Collection Development. We work together to explore funding opportunities for expensive purchases for the Reference Collection. Without special allocations Reference could not afford such additions as the cumulated volumes of the *Social Sciences Citation Index* or the new, revised microfiche catalog of the Bibliotheque Nationale. Each of our CD ROM products has had start-up funding from extramural funds. Reference now has *Dissertation Abstracts Ondisc*, the *Original Oxford English Dictionary on Compact Disc*, and the *MLA International Bibliography* on CD ROM. The *British Library General Catalogue of Printed Books to 1975* on CD ROM is on order.

I also meet weekly with the heads of the other divisions in the Reference Department. Our philosophy is that the Collection Development Division selects and evaluates reference sources and decides where they are housed. Collection Development interacts with the Reference Technical Services Division on the ordering, claiming, payment approval, and processing of the titles. Collection Development collaborates with the Public Services Division on how to best serve the public. The Division Chiefs participate as a management group and, with the Head of the Reference Department, form an administrative action team. There are also mechanisms for communication within the Collection Development Division. Every week I meet with the Assistant Head of the Collection Development Division, and every two weeks the entire Collection Development Division assembles. For day-to-day communication all reference librarians use electronic mail.

As stated earlier, our primary clientele is the UCLA faculty. They establish the programs, create the research topics, advise the graduate students, advance the scholarship, and, in effect, drive our collections. Through direct communication at the Reference Desk, bibliographic updates and lectures, monitoring interlibrary loan requests, interaction with bibliographers, reading journals, attending lectures and classes, and by keeping in touch through various other channels, librarians inform themselves on new and developing teaching and research needs. We have effective mechanisms for reaching out to faculty and students, and we are confident we have the structures in place for making the changes that will continue to make us responsive to them, our primary clientele. We look forward to the excitement of the new technology, surely to dominate acquisitions for the 1990s, and we are ready for an electrifying year 2000.

III. EVALUATING AND WEEDING COLLECTIONS

Discovering How Information Seekers Seek: Methods of Measuring Reference Collection Use

Mary Biggs

SUMMARY. The author observes that reference collections are often too large for librarians and users to learn them well and fully exploit them. Evidence suggests that many titles in what were designed to be lean "working" reference collections are rarely if ever consulted. Systematically-gathered use data are needed to guide selection and weeding decisions. Methods that have been employed to assess in-library materials use — including use of journals and circulating books as well as of reference works — are reviewed and their application to reference materials discussed. The author closes with concrete recommendations for carrying out reference collection use studies.

In an era when neither library budgets nor library buildings expand proportionately to the growth of publication, librarians need solid data to inform their collection decisions. Perhaps most needful

Mary Biggs was Assistant Professor in the Columbia University School of Library Service when this article was written. She is at present Director of Libraries, Mercy College, 555 Broadway, Dobbs Ferry, NY 10522.

and most neglected are reference librarians. Given their purpose, one would expect a library's reference works to comprise a lean "working" collection, well-known and thoroughly exploited by the reference staff. Additions to the collection would be made cautiously, and works that were rarely or never used would be weeded regularly for discarding or removal to another part of the library. Many reference librarians have, after all, remarked the critical need to "learn" the collection and the frustration of being defeated by its size.[1]

In late 1985, Victor Biggs and I surveyed reference heads in 471 academic libraries of all sizes.[2] We discovered that even within libraries of comparable size and purpose, the numbers of titles held in reference collections varied greatly. In all of our four size strata, including small college libraries, collections numbering tens of thousands of titles could be found.[3] And while all libraries weeded their reference collections, and substantial percentages indicated that "low use" by librarians or patrons was one weeding criterion, very few libraries had ever gathered use data systematically.[4] This was all the more striking as respondents estimated that only about one-fifth of the titles in their reference collections were used by anyone as often as once a month (with some guessing as low as 1%); that slightly under half were used annually (with some guesses as low as 5%); and that only about two-thirds were used in a five-year period (with guesses as low as 10%).[5]

These guesstimates, however, were just that. And even if they were accurate, a reader of the article pointed out to us in a letter, they would offer little guidance. The obstacle to whittling the collection into a lean mean reference tool lies in the difficulty of determining *which* 80% is not used once a month, *which* half is not used in a year, and *which* 30% lies idle for five years and more. This observation circles back to the need for use studies. How can they be carried out, and what can they tell us?

Precisely because there have been so few, the library literature offers little direct advice. To discover pertinent models, I examined reports of research on in-library use of all types of material, most prominently of periodicals. Here I summarize the principal research methods employed, consider their applicability, and set forth suggestions for multi-faceted explorations of reference-collection use.

TOUCH TECHNIQUES

Perhaps the easiest to implement are what Fussler and Simon call "all or nothing" studies.[6] Equating one use with many, these can at best yield only gross tabulations of works used, or moved, for any purpose in a given period. They are essentially of two types.

What can be termed the "Reach Out and Touch Technique" involves placing in each book (or in a selected sample of those books whose utility is doubted) some substance or item which will surely be disturbed if the book is moved. At the end of the study—which can extend over any period, though most likely a few months or a year—"disturbed" titles are noted. Among the substances that may be planted inconspicuously, Fussler and Simon suggest, are "infrared dust, beads on top of the book, or unexposed photographic paper inserted between the pages."[7] One portion of a periodical-use study at Newcastle University employed ordinary slips of paper.[8]

Obviously, the task of dusting, beading, or otherwise marking the books would be tedious and time-consuming, as would taking tallies to close the study (and sweeping up the beads before they tumbled readers to the floor). But a more substantive problem is the false registering as uses of mere physical disruptions. Books moved by shelvers to make space, or mistakenly pulled out by patrons misreading call numbers, or merely jostled by someone bumping against the stacks, may be recorded as "used." The great advantage of this technique, however, is its independence of reader cooperation. "It has been found," warns M. B. M. Campbell, "that the degree of success with any [use study] is inversely proportional to the level of user participation required by the methodology employed."[9]

RESHELVING TECHNIQUES

Reshelving techniques, which may or may not fall into the all-or-nothing category of research, require user participation but no user effort, and are probably the most popular methods because they can be integrated with normal library activity. Shelvers simply record items when putting them away. The variations are many, depending on the time available and just what the librarians wish to learn. At least in theory, all titles can be listed on a tally sheet ordered by call number or title, with space provided for the shelvers' hatch marks. Alternatively, shelvers can list the titles of works as they are re-shelved. But when tens of thousands of titles are involved, this will slow the shelving considerably.

W. M. Shaw, Jr. suggests affixing a small pressure-sensitive label to a book's spine the first time it is reshelved[10]—which is an all-or-nothing technique if the book is then ignored until the final tally. If the label is large enough to accommodate hatch marks, however, numbers of reshelvings can be recorded.[11] I used a related method when working at Bowling Green State University (Ohio). A small colored dot was pressed to the spine of each reference book the first time it was reshelved in a semester. This continued for two semesters and one summer, with dots of different colors used for each of the three time periods (i.e., fall semester was green, spring semester red, summer session silver). Although numbers of uses within a semester could not be told from this study, it did reveal whether the book was used consistently. When the study was completed, the subject specialists (all of whom also had reference and user education responsibilities) scanned the shelves in their call-number areas of expertise and noted those titles that had lain unused all year or had been used in only one semester. If a specialist wished to retain such a title in reference, he had to write a supporting rationale and have his request approved by the head of reference. A weeded title might be discarded, stored, put into circulation, or sent to the stacks as a non-circulating item—which guaranteed its availability in the building but reduced "noise" in the working reference collection. Obviously, a dot study could extend over a shorter or longer period: dots come in many colors.

Offsetting the simplicity and relative ease of reshelving studies are the fact that they cannot yield qualitative data and inevitably underestimate use. Everything depends upon used works being pulled off the shelf and left off. But unobtrusive observation and other checks on users' habits show that even when signs ask them not to do so, many people reshelve the books they consult, especially when they have used them for only a few minutes. At Newcastle University, for example, twenty-one of fifty-five periodicals that were used were also reshelved.[12] Discussing a periodicals use study, Martin Gordon asserts: "It should be noted in passing that some feel . . . uses [marked by the need to reshelve] are equalled or even exceeded by [other] uses, but that [the former] are more indicative of need fulfillment.''[13] Without supporting evidence, however, this is unduly optimistic and does not in any case deny the possibility of large distortions. To prevent patrons from reshelving, librarians customarily post signs asking them to leave materials at conveniently placed collection points, sometimes adding the explanation that a use study is underway.[14] The study may also be publicized through talks to user groups, announcements in campus or town newspapers, and so forth—though Edward T. Shearin warns that too much fanfare may make readers self-conscious about their library behavior and alter normal use patterns.[15]

Figures may also be deflated when two or more people use a book before it can be reshelved, scooping it up from a table or collection bin. To minimize this problem, the authors of the American Library Association's influential manual entitled *Output Measures for Public Libraries* recommend gathering data only on sample days, during which books are reshelved punctually every hour on the hour.[16]

A problem with opposite effect is the fact that an unshelved work may have received no more than a cursory glance from its "user" or have fallen accidentally when a neighboring volume was pulled down—may, in any case, represent no serious use, no satisfied need.

In short, though the data gleaned by shelvers can be valuable, it will ideally be supplemented with other methods.

USER TALLIES AND SELF-ADMINISTERED QUESTIONNAIRES

Relying much more on users' cooperation, yet a potentially rich source of qualitative data, is not-so-simply asking people what they use and how.

In a study of the periodical collection at the National Oceanic and Atmospheric Administration Library, Wenger and Childress attached to each current journal issue a slip of paper asking readers to make a check-mark if they use the issue "for any reason."[17] At Wolverhampton Polytechnic Library, Campbell placed punch-card sets in periodicals with the request that readers remove one card for each article consulted and place it (or them) in a handily located collection tray.[18] Because such techniques require little of the user, they are thought (but not known) to elicit high cooperation.

More interesting and problematic is the method employed by Fussler and Simon in their famous study of research library book use. Eschewing simple counts, this team sought to answer four questions: why the reader had removed the volume from its shelf; where and for what purpose he would use it; and how valuable he expected to find it.[19] In each sample book was placed a sheet of paper asking these questions. This questionnaire, which could not be seen unless the book was removed from the shelf, would be visibly disturbed if the book was opened – allowing the researchers to determine rate of nonresponse. That is, by counting questionnaires disturbed but not returned, they could tell how many people had used (or at least handled) a sample book but not filled out a questionnaire. In about half the sample books, cheap ballpoint pens were taped to the questionnaires, providing both an easy means of filling them out and a "reward." Readers returned many more of the questionnaires that had been accompanied by pens, which, according to the authors, "hints at the degree of caprice in motivation" and, of course, gives still more information about nonresponse. That is, it can be assumed that "at least as many questionnaires as the difference between the two groups were seen but not returned."[20] The disadvantage of the Fussler-Simon method is its complete reliance on reader cooperation, hence low response rate. However, it yields rich qualitative data. The questions asked, of course, would vary depending on the study's objective. In an investigation of reference book use, it would be helpful to know why the reader opened the work; whether and to what degree it was helpful; possibly whether, to the users' knowledge, another reference work would have sufficed; and, of course, the call number of the book in which he found the questionnaire. However, keeping the questions short, simple, and few would maximize response rate.

OTHER USER QUESTIONNAIRES AND INTERVIEWS

A related technique was used by Alice Bowen, who presented to randomly-selected readers in the stacks questionnaires asking about the next four books they touched.[21] Similarly, in the renowned University of Pittsburgh study, data collectors watched the library's journal area during scheduled periods and either interviewed or gave a questionnaire for completion to each journal user they spotted.[22] The danger lies in possibly making readers so self-conscious as to alter the use patterns they would have evinced otherwise. (In a reference collection, of course, where people often use only one or two titles, Bowen's technique can be modified to ask only about the book the reader is presently using, or the next *one*, rather than the next four, that he handles.)

A somewhat similar method was employed by Campbell partly to learn about journal use, partly to check the reliability of findings obtained using a different method. During a three-hour period in each of several months, library staff members questioned readers about the journals that they had been using.[23] This method could easily be applied to a study of reference-collection use, but the time periods would have to be selected carefully. To identify a single three-hour period that would be adequately representative seems impossible. Alternatively, several single hours or two-hour blocks could be randomly selected from the entire time that the reference collection was available to users throughout the month. Or sections of time believed to evince distinctive patterns of use might be identified—e.g., weekend days, weekday mornings, weekday afternoons, Sunday evenings, Monday evenings, other weekday evenings—and one or more hours selected randomly from within each section.

Similarly, ALA's *Output Measures . . .* manual suggests that users be approached as they leave the library and asked what materials they used.[24] Although people are usually much more likely to grant interviews than to complete questionnaires (a major advantage of interviewing), in this case timing may present a problem. That is, people often leave the library in a hurry, on the way to work, class, family, or social event—which can negatively affect response rate and, more important, the thoughtfulness and accuracy of the responses given.

Seeking to correlate in-house materials use patterns with types of user, one group of public libraries administered both questionnaires and interviews to adult patrons. They were asked not only what materials they had used and for what length of time each, but also their age, sex, occupation, level of education, and "primary reason for coming to the library." These activities were supplemented by reshelving counts, conducted according to recommendations in the *Output Measures . . .* manual; and by unobtrusive observation of library users, a technique discussed below.[25]

All methods involving the questioning of users pose the challenge of selecting not only representative time periods but representative users. Unless the study employs sufficient staff to approach *all* eligible users (e.g., all people in the reference area at the sample time, or all of those leaving the library), subjects must be selected in truly random fashion to avoid researcher bias. Otherwise, for example, people who appear especially friendly or unrushed will more likely be approached, and this can skew findings. Of course, if investigators wish to learn which sources are used by specific categories of user—by faculty, perhaps, or undergraduates, by retirees or high school students—then all users, or a random sample of users, who could conceivably fall into those categories must be approached and their eligibility for the study determined before questioning proceeds.

Justis and Wright administered a quite different kind of questionnaire to students in two graduate psychology classes at a college of education. A broad research question was articulated and the students asked which sources they would use to find pertinent information.[26] Although this particular study had extremely narrow scope, the technique can be adapted for use with faculty and students at all levels, in any and all disciplines, to discover which reference works they know about and are most likely to use.

Some academic librarians have, in fact, questioned faculty about which materials in certain categories they use and most highly value. For instance, McBride and Stenstrom asked University of Illinois social scientists which journals they "regularly read." The study's purpose was "to create guidelines that could be used to evaluate serial collection development."[27] Taking a subtly different approach, Wenger and Childress asked 452 scientists which journals were important enough to them, personally, for the library to maintain.[28] Interestingly, they found only a weak correlation between journals named and those which, in a complementary reshelving study, were found to be most often used. But the same technique applied to the reference collection would likely yield different results.

A. T. Murty, of India's Vikram University Library, sought more qualitative data when questioning "university teachers and research scholars" in physics and geology about their use of "bibliographical tools" (i.e., bibliographies, indexes, and abstracts). Through a written survey, he asked what they used and for what purposes, following up with interviews when it seemed desirable to probe their answers. Murty also used the opportunity to ask about problems of access and which changes in the library's services were most desired by the scientists.[29]

Multi-method studies were relatively uncommon because of their complexity, but they allow researchers to check on, and compensate for, the limitations of each individual method, avoiding distorted or simplistic conclusions and resultant bad decisions. Shearin, for example, followed a reshelving study of journals use at Central Piedmont Community College with a faculty survey. All journal titles were listed by academic department (with, of course, some overlap among departments); use figures derived from reshelving counts were provided for the titles. A librarian then visited each department and explained both the study itself and the figures. Using the lists, faculty members offered their recommendations for journal deletions, a list of suggested deletions was compiled, and the library staff reviewed them and made the final decisions. Shearin points out that not only were 13% of the library's journals cancelled, freeing funds to buy more urgently needed titles, but: "Meeting with the faculty and using their recommendations strengthened the library's public relations . . ."[30]

PROBLEMS OF QUESTIONNAIRING AND INTERVIEWING

For all their advantages, questionnairing and interviewing entail difficulties as well. Low questionnaire response rates and the need to identify representative times and respondents have already been mentioned, but the problems begin farther back. Creating a clear, valid questionnaire that will elicit easily interpreted answers – in written form or orally – is tougher than most people think and requires more time and expertise than many librarians have. Without going into all of the problems (they have been discussed elsewhere[31]), I will note one that is especially likely to bedevil research on library use. What do many of the words commonly found in questions mean? What is a "book"? A "reference work"? An "abstract"? An "index"? What constitutes a "use"? The list of potentially ambiguous terms seems endless. Rubin points out that in the public library study he reports, no definition was offered of "use," as in "using the library,"[32] although it seems susceptible to literally dozens of different interpretations. McBride and Stenstrom admit that when they queried faculty about "journals . . . regularly read," they left the definitions of all three terms up to each faculty member. Almost certainly, then, many apparently identical answers actually referred to different behaviors.[33] Murty notes that his scientist-respondents turned out to have no clear single idea of what a "bibliographical review" was, though it seemed plain enough to him.[34] Bookstein[35] and Kidston,[36] among others, have demonstrated and discussed the problem of definition, urging that clear, concrete explanations of all technical or ambitious terms be provided and questionnaires be carefully pilot tested.

Also, if answers depend at all upon memory — as when people are asked upon leaving the library what materials they used when there, or when students or faculty are asked what they habitually use or read — chances are good that some valued title will be forgotten, not mentioned.

Finally, the researcher must remember that most people prefer to be seen in a flattering light, even when what they say is registered anonymously. When being questionnaired or interviewed, a person is not rewarded for perfect truthfulness or penalized for white lies. Thus, for example, he may tend to overestimate the number of reference works he uses, or name those he considers most sophisticated whether or not he uses them often, while omitting or underemphasizing more-used but less impressive works.

Interviewing poses special challenges because, unless all interviewers are thoroughly, and identically, trained (and perhaps even if they are), they may bias responses through tone, attitude, gesture, facial expression, or adlibbed remarks. Also, if more than one interviewer participates, answers gleaned by the different interviewers may not be strictly comparable unless the questions are closed-ended and very straightforward. People respond differently to different people — are more or less verbose, more or less candid, based on often-subtle personal characteristics of those with whom they speak.

UNOBTRUSIVE OBSERVATION

When using this technique, the researcher is witness, no longer dependent upon what people remember or understand or want him to believe, or on their attentiveness to signs and willingness to leave books in sloppy piles. But this great advantage is balanced by the time and training that observation requires, and by the danger that users may realize they are being watched and somehow modify their behavior accordingly, perhaps leaving the area altogether. Also, hours for observation, like hours for in-library questionnairing and interviewing, must be selected carefully and systematically so that the resulting data will describe representative use patterns.

GATHERING DATA FROM LIBRARIANS

The reference collection, unlike materials elsewhere in the library, is used not only by patrons themselves but by librarians on their behalf. This is, of course, a major reason for having a segregated reference collection at all, usually clustered in the vicinity of the reference librarians' public station. So it is at least equally important to determine what the librarians use.

They, like patrons, can be questionnaired or interviewed, though the approach and the questions will differ. But a simpler technique is the librarian tally, which requires librarians to record the titles they use, either by listing them or, more efficiently, by drawing hatch marks on a prepared alphabetical title list. The information yielded is valuable, and the task of marking a prepared list, though annoying at a busy reference desk, is not really much more time-consuming than the type-of-question tallies that are commonly kept.

James B. Woy reports a survey variation on the title tally. In his study, which sought to determine public and academic librarians' level of use of the various looseleaf business reference sources, 139 librarians were mailed questionnaires listing the sources and asking whether each was consulted "frequently," "moderately" often, or "seldom."[37] Unfortunately, those terms were not defined, so it is impossible to interpret the answers. But certainly a researcher *could* incorporate definitions of frequency into such a questionnaire.

IN CONCLUSION

Each method described here, and any other conceivable method of assessing reference collection use, is inherently limited. Librarians may seize upon these limitations and resist assessment altogether. More sensibly, they may identify the *strengths* of each type of study, decide which—and with what modifications—best suits their needs and resources, and plan such a study, bearing in mind its limitations and avoiding the temptation to draw conclusions inadequately supported by their findings. When possible, librarians may devise several approaches to the problem of assessment in order to acquire complementary sets of data, check the reliability of their findings, or both. For example, a reshelving study may be followed by a survey of faculty reactions; or interviews with reference-area patrons and tallies by librarians of personal use may be carried out concurrently with a "touch" count. And probably the research project will have to be designed so that it, or elements of it, can be carried out continuously or repeated at appropriate intervals.

The methodological possibilities are many and choices will vary based on a library's goals, problems, reference collection characteristics, and available time, money, imagination, and expertise. Of these four always-scarce items, the last two may be the most elusive. But the abundant literature of empirical research methodology and statistics can help, as can local researchers and statisticians on campus or in the community who may be persuaded to donate advice. If no such Samaritans are to be found, a library may be forced to hire paid consultants. Considering the vast time and effort consumed by any evaluation project (and often underestimated in advance), eschewing purchased expertise in order to economize may turn out to be costly indeed.

So, even more certainly, will flat refusal to evaluate. As paper reference works pile up around us, threatening landslide at any moment, and online databases and compact disk services proliferate, charming us and dizzying us at once, we must distinguish what we need from what we do not, what we simply like from what we cannot serve without. Only then can we make fully rational decisions about how to spend our money, allot our space, direct our energy.

REFERENCES

1. See, for example: Mary Lou Goodyear, "Are We Losing Control at the Reference Desk?: A Reexamination," *RQ* 25 (Fall 1985): 85; Charles A. Bunge, "Potential and Reality at the Reference Desk: Reflections on a 'Return to the Field,'" *Journal of Academic Librarianship* 10 (July 1984): 129; and William Miller, "What's Wrong with Reference?: Coping with Success and Failure at the Reference Desk," *American Libraries* 15 (May 1984): 303.

2. Mary Biggs and Victor Biggs, "Reference Collection Development in Academic Libraries: Report of a Survey," *RQ* 27 (Fall 1987): 67-79.

3. The ranges were: college libraries, 275-35,000 titles; libraries in Master's- (but not doctoral-) granting institutions, 5,000-85,000 titles; libraries in doctoral-granting institutions not belonging to the Association for Research Libraries (ARL), 900-60,000 titles; and ARL libraries, 5,000-82,000 titles (Biggs and Biggs, p. 69).

4. Only five (7%) of college libraries, 9 (11%) of libraries in Master's-granting institutions, 5 (11%) of libraries in doctoral-granting institutions, and 4 (6%) of ARL libraries had conducted reference-collection use studies (Biggs and Biggs, p. 74).

5. These figures are drawn from the means shown on Table 8 in Biggs and Biggs, p. 75.

6. Herman H. Fussler and Julian L. Simon, *Patterns in the Use of Books in Large Research Libraries* (Chicago: University of Chicago Press, 1969): 108.

7. Ibid.

8. Robert Broadus, "The Measurement of Periodicals Use," *Serials Review* 11 (Summer 1985): 57-61.

9. M. B. M. Campbell, "A Survey of the Use of Science Periodicals in Wolverhampton Polytechnic Library," *Research in Librarianship* 5 (May 1974): 42.

10. W. M. Shaw, Jr., "A Practical Journal Usage Technique," *College and Research Libraries* 39 (November 1978): 479-84.

11. Blaine H. Hall, *Collection Assessment Manual for College and University Libraries* (Phoenix, AZ: Oryx Press, 1985): 67.

12. Broadus. See also: Charles B. Wenger and Judith Childress, "Journal Evaluation in a Research Library," *Journal of the American Society for Information Science* 28 (September 1977): 293-99.

13. Martin Gordon, "Periodicals Use at a Small College Library," *Serials Librarian* 6 (Summer 1982): 64.

14. For examples of reshelving studies and sign wording, see: Wenger and Childress; Carolyn M. Moore and Linda Mielke, "Taking the Measure: Applying Reference Outputs to Collection Development," *Public Libraries* 25 (Fall 1986): 108-11; Nancy P. Johnson, "Legal Periodical Usage Survey: Methods and Application," *Law Library Journal* 71 (February 1978): 177-86; and Edward F. Shearin, Jr., "Journal Usage Survey," *North Carolina Libraries* 34 (Summer 1976): 9-10.

15. Shearin, p. 10.

16. Nancy A. Van House et al., *Output Measures for Public Libraries: A Manual of Standardized Procedures*, 2d ed. (Chicago: American Library Association, 1987): 45.

17. Wenger and Childress. See also: D. Eardley and R. F. Eatwell, "Surveys of Journal Use in the Library of the University of Surrey, 1972-1975: A Methodology," in *Proceedings of the Seventh Meeting of IATUL, Leuven, May 16-21, 1977*, edited by Nancy Fjallbrant and Kerstin McCarthy (Goteborg, Sweden: IATUL, Chalmers University of Technology Library, 1978): 161-65.

18. Campbell, pp. 42-43.

19. Fussler and Simon, p. 172.

20. Fussler and Simon, p. 110.

21. Alice Bowen, "Nonrecorded Use of Books and Browsing in the Stacks of a Research Library," (M.A. thesis, University of Chicago, 1961).

22. Roger Flynn, "Use of Journals," in *Use of Library Materials: The University of Pittsburgh Study*, by Allen Kent et al. (New York: Marcel Dekker, 1979): 61.

23. Campbell, p. 24.

24. Van House et al., p. 47.

25. Richard Rubin, "Measuring the In-House Use of Materials in Public Libraries," *Public Libraries* 25 (Winter 1986): 137-38.

26. Lorraine Justis and Janet Schuman Wright, "Who Knows What? What?" *RQ* 12 (Winter 1972): 172-74.

27. Ruth B. McBride and Patricia Stenstrom, "Psychology Journal Usage," *Behavioral and Social Sciences Librarian* 2 (Fall 1980/1981): 1-12.

28. Wenger and Childress, p. 296.

29. A. T. Murty, "Use of Bibliographical Tools," *Indian Librarian* 26 (March 1972): 182-86.

30. Shearin, p. 10.

31. See, for example: Ronald R. Powell, *Basic Research Methods for Librarians* (Norwood, NJ: Ablex, 1985): 89-108; Seymour Sudman and Norman M. Bradburn, *Asking Questions* (San Francisco: Jossey-Bass, 1982); Norman M. Bradburn and Seymour Sudman, *Improving Interview Method and Questionnaire Design* (San Francisco: Jossey-Bass, 1979); and Stanley L. Payne, *The Art of Asking Questions* (Princeton, NJ: Princeton University Press, 1980 [copyright 1951]).

32. Rubin, p. 138.

33. McBride and Stenstrom, p. 3.

34. Murty, p. 183.

35. Abraham Bookstein, "Questionnaire Research in a Library Setting," *Journal of Academic Librarianship* 11 (March 1985): 24-28; and Abraham Bookstein, "Sources of Error in Library Questionnaires," *Library Research* 4 (Spring 1982): 85-94.

36. James S. Kidston, "The Validity of Questionnaire Responses," *Library Quarterly* 55 (April 1985): 133-50.

37. James B. Woy, "Loose Leaf Business Services," *RQ* 9 (Fall 1969): 128-33.

"Use" as a Criterion for the Weeding of Reference Collections: A Review and Case Study

Eugene A. Engeldinger

SUMMARY. Very little has been published about weeding reference collections until the past few years and very little of that has been empirical research. The literature on the subject is reviewed here with emphasis on use of the material as a condition for deselection. The University of Wisconsin, Eau Claire Library has collected data for five years; this data is used to show that even in well weeded collections, which previously depended upon subjective methods, empirical data will prove beneficial. Proper reference collection management requires more than subjective judgments. Empirical data may provide a number of surprises. Data collection is being made easier by automation.

INTRODUCTION

The two essential elements of the successful reference department are the reference staff and the reference collection. To provide excellent service it is necessary that both be of excellent quality. Until recently there has been little published research regarding the use that items in the reference collection actually receive. Much has been written regarding the development of a good library collection and how to select those materials that would be of greatest importance to the users. Until the past few years, however, there has been almost no research available about collection development policies or the elimination of material from academic library reference collections.

Eugene A. Engeldinger is Head of Public Services, McIntyre Library, University of Wisconsin, Eau Claire, WI 54702-4004.

Two recently conducted surveys of U.S. academic libraries[1] confirm that few have written collection development policies and even fewer have written weeding policies. It is generally accepted that reference materials have characteristics unique from other types of books that encourage their being shelved together. Among these is the type, and sometimes frequency, of use the materials are expected to receive. This anticipated use is important in determining whether the books are placed in the reference collection or with the general circulating stacks. Books that are consulted frequently for only small portions of their total volume are deemed "reference."[2] Usually it is believed that a greater number of library users would be inconvenienced by the absence of these books from the shelves than the number of users who would benefit by a policy which allowed their circulation.

This assumption of possible frequency, and sometimes urgency, of need is a major factor in restricting reference book circulation and giving these materials prime library space. Logic would dictate that if an item turns out to receive little or no use, it should lose its reference status. If an item is not consulted as frequently as originally anticipated, even if it is a "reference" type, reference staff should consider transferring it to the stacks or discarding it.

SHELF SPACE

Weeding might not be necessary if the library has plenty of room in its reference area. Some librarians might argue that if a book is not heavily used while in reference, it probably would not receive any more use in the stacks. In fact, some might argue, it would receive even less use there. At least one study, however, indicates that shelf space in reference departments is not in ample supply. In that study it was revealed that fifty percent of the respondents believed they had two years or less space in reference at current rates of acquisition.[3] Seventy-five percent believed they had four years or less. This situation leaves little doubt that the question of weeding cannot be ignored and, undoubtedly, is not.

CRISIS WEEDING

In all likelihood what occurs in most libraries is what might be called "crisis weeding." That is, librarians select new materials and add them without reviewing the shelves for deselection. When a certain area of the collection becomes too full and there is no more room for new acquisitions, decisions are made regarding what is least essential; these items are then weeded, the number depending upon how much room is required. We believe there is also a tendency to deselect the thicker volumes or the multi-volume sets since this action will net the most space with the least effort. Sometimes shelf shifting will temporarily relieve the tight spots, but for many collections that option too is short lived.

An important component in this crisis weeding is perceived use of the material in the crowded section. The new items are expected to receive greater use, thus they should be allocated reference space. Guestimates must be made regarding which of the older volumes will receive less use; these are then weeded. Use, or anticipated use, will weigh heavily in this decision making.

Interestingly enough, a sort of inequity develops. Since the shelves are so full, no shifting can be done. Those areas with the greatest activity will be the prime targets for eliminating the least used volumes, while less active areas are likely to be untouched. For example class "Z" schedule volumes might be receiving less use and therefore are kept in place since no crisis exists there, while more heavily used items in the "PR" classification must be weeded because of the acquisition of newer titles. The irony is that moderately used volumes are forced out of reference while unused items stay, merely because no shelf space is available where it is needed.

SURVEYS OF THE IMPORTANCE OF USE

In both the Biggs and the Engeldinger studies, respondents were asked what role use of material plays in their weeding program. In Engeldinger's 1982 survey with 377 responses, slightly over half indicated that "frequency of use" was a consideration for weeding.[4] That's nearly half of the respondents saying use was *not* considered. The 1985 Biggs study shows that about three-quarters of their 471 responses considered low use by librarians, or by faculty, as reasons for weeding.[5] Between one-third and one-half of the respondents considered both types of use in their decision making. The conclusion to be drawn from these surveys is that between one-fourth and one-half of reference librarians do *not* include the use which an item has received when they consider it for withdrawal.

In both studies it was discovered that the level of use was determined by informal observation and staff judgments. Biggs found that fewer than 10 percent brought any empirical data to bear on their decisions.[6] In Engeldinger's study only 23 of the 377 respondents admitted to conducting any kind of use study and none shared the results or described the process.[7] When Biggs' respondents were asked to estimate *how much* of their collection was used, they suggested that less than half of the reference works were consulted once or more annually and that over 30 percent of the materials in their collections were used less than once in five years.[8] If true, these collections would be greatly improved if the unused items could be identified.

Several articles have appeared recently in the literature that give advice about criteria to apply when withdrawing books from the reference collection. Adalian and Rockman[9] recommend a title-by-title review, but nowhere is there any indication that frequency of use is considered. In Westbrook's essay consideration of use level is implied but not stated.[10] In both cases, as well as with Nichols' article,[11] anticipated or potential use seems to be the guide. In none of these writings did the authors express the desirability of collecting empirical data, although it is doubtful that they would favor ignoring use data were it available. They undoubtedly reflect the attitude of most reference librarians that use data is too difficult to gather or that it is unnecessary. Reducing the number of titles to about one-third of its original size as was done by Adalian and Rockman certainly is a noteworthy, and perhaps enviable, achievement.[12] We wonder how much more (or less) would have been weeded if empirical use data had been brought to bear on the deliberation.

The only empirical study of academic reference collection use was published recently by Arrigona and Mathews. The purpose of the study was to determine which parts of the collection received greatest use and whether the use habits of librarians differed from those of patrons.[13] No attempt was made to determine the number of uses for a particular item; rather, the authors hoped to learn use frequency of certain call number areas. The table count method was adopted with use being defined as having occurred if an item had to be reshelved. The table count was conducted over a four week period in Spring Semester 1986.

UWEC—A CASE STUDY

At the University of Wisconsin-Eau Claire we have been collecting data for several years on use of our reference collection. The project was begun in an attempt to determine which areas of the collection were most heavily used, and which specific volumes within those areas. Up to that time the reference collection had been reviewed annually, title-by-title, with the pulled volumes given additional evaluation by the other reference staff. The preliminary deselection was done by the same person in an attempt to be as consistent as possible. Although unwritten, the criteria consisted of remembered use, probable past and future use, judgment that an item *should* be used even if it had not been, and perception of inconvenience to users if an item was transferred to the stacks and subsequently checked out. During the same procedure, certain volumes were earmarked for replacement by newer editions or suitable surrogates, replacement of missing or illegible labels, missing pages, rebinding and other repairs.

Over the years this had created what we perceived to be a trim and well-used collection. Nonetheless, there was a suspicion that some empirical evidence of use would be valuable to us. Thus it was decided to gather as much data as possible regarding actual use of the reference materials.

SPINE-MARKING

A reading of Slote[14] convinced us that a variation on the spine marking method was probably the best for measuring use of a non-circulating collection. We conceded it would be imprecise data, but some evidence of use would be more valuable than what we had to date, which were mostly impressions and wishful thinking. We decided that items requiring reshelving would be counted as having been used. Of course, the problems with this definition are obvious and have been addressed by other writers. Nonetheless it does allow us to make decisions and take action.

The student shelvers were trained to place a stick-on dot inside the back cover of every reference book they reshelved. We decided a limit of five dots for fear that with some titles, the whole inside would be filled within several months. Five uses were judged to be sufficiently high; knowledge of more use was unnecessary for our purposes.

"Dotting" began in August 1981, at the beginning of the Fall semester. The original plan had been to collect data for a semester or two, but because applying the dots took little extra effort and did little to disrupt our routines, it was continued until 1986. The time requirements for counting the dots was another story, however. There was never enough student assistant funding in the regular budget to survey the entire collection, but, fortunately during some years, special funds were made available by university administration or other local agencies for various projects, and we were able to take advantage of them.

During the summer of 1986 the dots were counted thereby providing us with data regarding five years of reference collection use. Figure 1 provides a summary of those data in a way that can be applied to policy making for our collection. We are now able to determine how much of the total reference collection is used, and how frequently, up to five times for the five-year period. We are able also to determine how much use various class numbers receive. In our situation this is extremely useful since our shelves are full, for all intents and purposes, with no room for expansion.

DECIDING ON ACCEPTABLE FREQUENCY OF USE

Among the first decisions we now must make is a determination of an acceptable frequency of use for a book to remain in Reference. Slote calls this the book's shelf life, that is, the length of time between uses. Each library must evaluate its own circumstances and

	0 Uses		1 Use		2 Uses		3 Uses		4 Uses		5 Uses		1-5 Uses		Total Vols. in Classification
A	90	50%	25	14%	12	7%	11	6%	8	4%	33	18%	89	50%	179
B-BF	47	34%	15	11%	6	4%	7	5%	12	9%	51	37%	91	66%	138
BH-BZ	45	16%	53	18%	39	14%	25	9%	30	10%	95	33%	242	84%	287
C	51	26%	42	21%	35	18%	16	8%	10	5%	46	23%	149	75%	200
D	176	32%	89	16%	72	13%	46	8%	35	6%	136	25%	378	68%	554
E	158	46%	64	18%	37	11%	26	7%	12	3%	50	14%	189	54%	347
F	42	25%	17	10%	13	8%	12	7%	10	6%	75	44%	127	75%	169
G	48	12%	35	9%	34	9%	38	10%	34	9%	198	51%	339	88%	387
H-HF	58	12%	61	13%	40	8%	48	10%	37	8%	244	50%	430	88%	488
HG-HZ	373	41%	153	17%	87	10%	58	6%	39	4%	190	21%	527	59%	900
J	112	32%	54	15%	42	12%	28	8%	22	6%	95	27%	241	68%	353
K	491	52%	175	19%	90	10%	64	7%	50	5%	74	8%	453	48%	944
L	60	16%	35	9%	31	8%	22	6%	31	8%	194	52%	313	84%	373
M	132	31%	72	17%	52	12%	24	6%	24	6%	122	29%	294	69%	426
N	65	30%	37	17%	27	12%	20	9%	22	10%	47	22%	153	70%	218
P-PN	270	24%	154	14%	104	9%	85	8%	92	8%	402	36%	837	76%	1107
PQ-PZ	138	41%	61	18%	47	14%	23	7%	18	5%	51	15%	200	59%	338
Q	152	29%	85	16%	57	11%	50	10%	38	7%	137	26%	367	71%	519
R	41	25%	29	18%	14	9%	10	6%	13	8%	57	35%	123	75%	164
S	17	24%	14	19%	8	11%	2	3%	7	10%	24	33%	55	76%	72
T	105	27%	74	19%	38	10%	28	7%	26	7%	125	32%	291	73%	396
UV	3	9%	8	25%	7	22%	3	9%	2	6%	9	28%	29	91%	32
Z	1072	49%	438	20%	219	10%	125	6%	89	4%	233	11%	1104	51%	2176
Totals	3746	34.8	1790	16.6	1111	10.3	771	7.1	661	6.1	2688	24.9	7021	65.2	10767

EAE4/UseChart: 1986

FIGURE 1. Numbers and Percentages of Use by Classification Numbers after 5 Years

reach a decision based upon local user needs, shelf space, curriculum requirements, budget, size of collection and other relevant factors. Our decision might well be, for example, that all volumes that have no recorded use after five years should be weeded. (Many items that old can probably be weeded anyway, but since we know this book was never used, we might decide that a new edition should go to the stacks, if purchased at all.)

If we set the acceptable use level for an item to remain in reference at one use in five years, we could eliminate about one-third of the titles, thus freeing up considerable shelf space. However, one might argue that keeping a book that had only one recorded use in five years was unjustifiable. Thus, if as a rule of thumb we said that reference materials must be used twice or more in five years, we could withdraw over half (51.4 percent) of the collection. While this would "demolish" the current collection, the relevant question to be addressed is whether such heavy weeding will cause the users of reference materials any serious inconvenience. Assuming we can trust the data, it is hard to believe the answer would be in the affirmative. One immediate benefit would be the ease with which one could find the "good stuff," undistracted by the "junk."

Many reference librarians from other institutions might believe such action would be too severe for *their* collections. Without this project we might never have realized so much of *our* material was used so infrequently. This would have been especially difficult to believe since we have had an ongoing weeding program which kept the reference stacks "lean and mean."

Putting our data into chart form allows us to see which *classes* of books receive the heaviest and lightest use. Most of us at UWEC have a feeling for where the activity is, but now we have a more precise awareness. We were surprised to learn, for example, that only half the books in the class "A" schedule are used. Our law section, which we have never deemed adequate, provided us with another surprise. Slightly more than half of the "K's" also are unused.

With this system of use recording and data collection we have another important ingredient for good collection management. Not only do we now know that about half of the collection has high potential for weeding, the dots (or lack thereof) let us know exactly which specific items are expendable. Some librarians may believe they already know which items are used and which are not. Perhaps, but in our case, reviewing the collection title-by-title, noting the dots, provided a number of surprises. Many items we thought were not used often, had been, while some that we believed would be popular when we purchased them turned out to be of little interest to users.

CONCLUSION

Some librarians may argue that such data collection is too time consuming, too tedious and the benefits not worth the efforts expended. These individuals might keep in mind that increasingly, particularly in libraries with automated systems, there are alternative methods of developing these records. Automation will make it easier to record in-house use and determine how much of the collection is active, whole call number areas as well as individual items. In any case, generation of useful empirical data takes several years and while some librarians might be inclined to await automation, we would caution against it. To properly manage a library, data is necessary. Imprecise use records are often superior to no data at all, especially when used cautiously. We have found such data to be superior to our previous reliance on memory of use and subjective judgment.

REFERENCES

1. Biggs, Mary and Victor Biggs. "Reference Collection Development in Academic Libraries: Report of a Survey." *RQ* 27 (Fall 1987): 67-79; Engeldinger, Eugene A. "Weeding of Academic Library Reference Collections: A Survey of Current Practice." *RQ* 25 (Spring 1986): 366-371.

2. For an excellent look at defining the nature of a reference book, see Bates, Marcia J. "What is a Reference Book? A Theoretical and Empirical Analysis." *RQ* 26 (Fall 1986): 37-57.

3. Engeldinger, p.369-70.

4. Engeldinger, p.371.

5. Biggs, p.74.

6. Biggs, p.74.

7. Engeldinger, p.371.

8. Biggs, p.74.

9. Adalian, Paul T. and Ilene F. Rockman. "Title-by-Title Review in Reference Collection Development." *RSR/Reference Services Review* 12 (Winter 1984): 85-88.

10. Westbrook, Lynn. "Weeding Reference Serials." *The Serials Librarian* 10 (Summer 1986): 81-100.

11. Nichols, Margaret Irby. "Weeding the Reference Collection." *Texas Library Journal* 62 (Winter 1986): 204-206.

12. Adalian and Rockman, p.87.

13. Arrigona, Daniel R. and Eleanor Mathews. "A Use Study of an Academic Library Reference Collection." *RQ* 28 (Fall 1988): 73.

14. Slote, Stanley J. *Weeding Library Collections-II*. 2nd rev. ed. Littleton, Colorado: Libraries Unlimited, Inc., 1982.

BIBLIOGRAPHY

Adalian, Paul T., Jr. and Ilene F. Rockman. "Title-by-Title Review in Reference Collection Development." *RSR/Reference Services Review* 12 (Winter 1984): 85-88.

Arrigona, Daniel R. and Eleanor Mathews. "A Use Study of an Academic Library Reference Collection." *RQ* 28 (Fall 1988): 71-81.

Bates, Marcia J. "What is a Reference Book? A Theoretical and Empirical Analysis." *RQ* 26 (Fall 1986): 37-57.

Biggs, Mary and Victor Biggs. "Reference Collection Development in Academic Libraries: Report of a Survey." *RQ* 27 (Fall 1987): 67-79.

Engeldinger, Eugene A. "Weeding of Academic Library Reference Collections: A Survey of Current Practice." *RQ* 25 (Spring 1986): 366-371.

Nichols, Margaret Irby. "Weeding the Reference Collection." *Texas Library Journal* 62 (Winter 1986): 204-6.

Rettig, James. "Love Canal in the Reference Stacks." *RSR/Reference Services Review* 10 (Winter 1982): 7.

Schlachter, Gail. "Obsolescence, Weeding, and Bibliographic Love Canals." *RQ* 28 (Fall 1988): 7-8.

Slote, Stanley J. *Weeding Library Collection-II*. 2nd rev. ed. Littleton, Colorado: Libraries Unlimited, Inc., 1982.

Westbrook, Lynn. "Weeding Reference Serials." *The Serials Librarian* 10 (Summer 1986): 81-100.

A Program for the Systematic Weeding of the Reference Collection

Eleanor Mathews
David A. Tyckoson

Weeding is defined as the process of removing materials which are no longer useful from a library collection. This process, which may be called deselection, deacquisition, book retirement, or pruning, is an essential yet often ignored component of collection management. Weeding is considered an integral part of the collection development program by the authors of standard collection development texts such as Evans[1] and Stueart and Miller,[2] but it is not often put into actual practice.

REASONS FOR WEEDING LIBRARY COLLECTIONS

Weeding must be an activity that is carried out to meet the specific collection objectives of an individual library. Different types of libraries will necessarily have different types of collections and will thus pursue different types of weeding programs. The collections of educational institutions support the curriculum offered by the institution, college and university libraries support the research efforts conducted by the faculty, public libraries support the information and recreational needs of their citizens, special libraries support the goals of their specific constituency, and national libraries serve as repositories for the knowledge and culture of mankind. Weeding should be a part of the collection management plan in all types of libraries. In *Weeding Library Collections II*, Slote[3] ob-

Eleanor Mathews is Head, Reference Department, 152 Parks Library, Iowa State University, Ames, IA 50011. David A. Tyckoson is a librarian at Iowa State University, 33 Parks Library, Ames, IA 50011.

129

serves that weeding does not reduce the ability of the library to meet these objectives, but "On the contrary, weeding seems to increase accessibility, improve efficiency, reduce costs, and in many other ways improve collections and services to the average user."

In many libraries, space is the primary criterion for beginning a weeding project. The time to weed comes when it is evident that there will be a shortage of shelf space to house newly acquired titles. Lucker[4] observes that "what is kept, for how long, and where are the principal questions that drive the development of a weeding policy for the MIT libraries." Those materials selected to remain on the open shelves should be those that are most likely to be used. In many libraries, materials that are weeded are not totally removed from the collection but are transferred to a storage area or other facility where they can still be retrieved quickly when requested.[5]

Weeding can actually enhance a library's collection. The overall appearance of the collection generally improves with weeding because the shelves are no longer crowded with unused, obsolete, or damaged books. Once the older materials have been removed, circulation often increases because it becomes easier to find the newer and more up-to-date sources.

Despite the advantages that have been identified from a weeding program, weeding of the library collection is not done for a number of reasons. Other professional tasks, many considered more interesting than weeding, allow little time for making decisions regarding the removal of materials from the collection. The staff time required to evaluate materials, change records, and physically move volumes to other locations can be considerable. In addition, one of the criteria used to evaluate libraries on a national level is the number of volumes contained in the collection. If a collection is reduced in size, the official volume count may also be reduced. This may affect the status and funding level of the library within its user community. Other reasons for not weeding include a reluctance to remove materials that were deemed worthy of selection in the first place, the possibility that rare works may be discarded, that the materials will be requested subsequent to being weeded, and that weeding constitutes "irresponsible destruction of public property."[6]

WEEDING OF THE REFERENCE COLLECTION

While weeding should be an essential component of any collection development program, it is especially important for the reference collection. Due to the inherent nature of reference materials, it is vital that the reference collection be constantly maintained and updated. This maintenance involves both the constant identification of new materials to be added to the collection and the constant removal of materials that are no longer of value. Most reference librarians vigorously pursue the first of these two objectives, but many neglect the second. Even with the best possible acquisition policy, reference collections tend to lose their value unless materials are removed when they no longer provide current and complete reference information.

In order to fully understand the importance of reference weeding, it is necessary to examine the relationship between the reference collection and the general library collection. The general collection in most libraries serves as the repository for original source materials in the subject fields of interest to the users of that library. These source materials usually include both current and historical information sources. Materials that are kept in the general collection usually remain as a part of that collection for a considerable length of time. While some of these materials may be in high demand, most of the sources contained in this part of the library are not consulted on a frequent basis.

Reference works, on the other hand, are those sources that either index or summarize the information provided in the general collection. The two most common types of reference sources are those that provide brief factual information, such as encyclopedias, dictionaries, almanacs, and handbooks, and those that refer the user to sources containing additional information, such as indexes, abstracts, and directories. Most reference sources are organized to provide the user with brief information on a rapid basis. While the exact subject matter of the sources contained within the reference collection will vary from library to library, in each case the primary role of the reference collection is to index and summarize the information contained in the general collection of that particular library.

As new information becomes available, it often replaces, supersedes, or contradicts information that existed previously. If the reference collection is to effectively index and summarize other information sources, this collection needs to be both comprehensive and timely in nature. To fulfill this objective, new information must constantly be added and old information must constantly be withdrawn. Reference librarians need to be critical not only in their evaluations of potential new purchases, but also in evaluating those sources already contained in the reference collection.

Unfortunately, little has been written about the weeding of reference collections. Guidelines for weeding specific types of materials, such as encyclopedias, almanacs, dictionaries, and handbooks, have been suggested. Nichols[7] recommends developing weeding policies by source type and also observes that "the systematic removal of that which is obsolete or inaccurate is an essential process for maintaining an effective reference collection." Westbrook provides an extensive list of titles for each type of reference source and recommends retention policies for each of them.[8]

A survey of the weeding policies of academic library reference collections has been conducted by Engeldinger.[9] Of the 377 colleges and universities responding to his questionnaire, he found that 11.9% had a written weeding policy and that 19% had unwritten weeding procedures for their reference collections. Over 81% of the reference departments surveyed had unwritten weeding practices, indicating that many reference departments do weed even though they do not have any specific guidelines, either written or unwritten. About one-half of the libraries (48.6%) weed systematically on a continuous basis, which was defined as more frequently than once every two years. The age of the material or the existence of a newer edition were found to be the two most common criteria for weeding. The usage of the material is not used as a deselection guideline, with few departments gathering empirical evidence for making such a judgement.

Biggs and Biggs[10] found in their survey on reference collection development that about one-fourth of the institutions they asked had developed written weeding policies. More libraries used a limit on the size of the collection to determine when weeding was appropriate, rather than relying on a formal weeding policy. The reference librarians surveyed thought that less than 70% of the materials in their reference collections were used as often as once every five years.

Weeding is beginning to become recognized as an important component of reference collection development. In the past seven years, editorials in two of the premier library science journals have commented on the danger of retaining obsolete material in the reference collection.[11] Schlachter goes on to suggest that the American Library Association's Reference and Adult Services Division take a leadership role in encouraging reference departments to develop a systematic approach to collection management.[12]

PHILOSOPHIES OF REFERENCE COLLECTION DEVELOPMENT

Two distinct philosophies of reference collection development have become prevalent among reference librarians. These two philosophies have been a topic of heated debate at conferences.[13] Most reference collections exist under a combination of these two concepts, although one philosophy usually prevails. The first states that all works of a reference nature should be kept in the reference collection. This theory is generally based upon the theory that patrons expect to find sources such as handbooks, dictionaries, and encyclopedias in the reference collection. Under this philosophy, format is the primary criterion for the identification of material for the reference collection. Reference collections built upon this philosophy tend to be large and comprehensive.

The second common philosophy of reference collection development states that the reference collection exists primarily for the use of the reference librarians in responding to reference queries. Under this philosophy, usage of the material is the primary criterion for selection of reference materials. On this basis, those sources that are not consulted by the reference librarians on a frequent basis should be housed in the general library collection, regardless of their format. Handbooks, encyclopedias, and dictionaries on topics that are not of primary interest to most of the library's users would normally be found in the circulating collection. Under this theory, sources that are used infrequently are made available in the circulating collection for those few patrons who are seeking them.

Weeding is especially important under the second of these two philosophies. If the collection exists primarily to serve the librarians in answering questions, that collection must provide the librarians with the sources necessary to carry out that function. It must also NOT include sources that provide outdated or incorrect information. Librarians operating under this philosophy must constantly update their collections in order to provide the latest and most complete information sources. They must also constantly scrutinize the collection and deselect materials that are no longer current, accurate, or frequently consulted by the reference librarians. Over the years, the concept of the reference collection at Iowa State University has migrated from following the first philosophy stated above to following the second. It is under this second policy that the systematic weeding program is based.

Under this philosophy, the reference collection should maintain a fairly stable number of titles. The goal of the reference librarian should be to provide those sources that provide the best and most recent information rather than a large number of sources that are all less than adequate. Without a systematic weeding policy, the useful works contained in many reference collections can become buried by a large quantity of old and insufficient sources. One way to avoid this problem is to maintain a no growth policy for the reference collection. A no growth policy forces the librarian to be very critical in evaluating potential reference sources. When selecting new sources to be added to the collection, all new reference sources must be better (under one of the criteria listed below) than the existing titles already in the collection. And whenever a new title is selected for addition to the collection, the old title that has been replaced should be transferred out of the collection. Although the total volume count will inevitably grow as new volumes are added to existing runs of subscriptions and as new sources are published that cover topics not already met by the collection, a no growth policy implies that a new title should replace an old title whenever possible.

One of the greatest concerns of reference librarians regarding the weeding process is that the information weeded from the reference collection will no longer be available if and when it is needed. This fear is based upon the assumption that once the reference source has been removed from the reference collection it will no longer be available to the librarian or the user. However, most materials weeded from the reference collection are not completely removed from the library, but become a part of the general circulating collection. These sources will still be a part of the total library collection and will continue to be available to both the librarian and the patron. As the indexing of the total library collection becomes more complete, particularly with the use of online catalogs, these materials will be almost as convenient for the reference librarian to identify and retrieve as those materials contained within the reference collection itself. As the information migrates from the core to more general sources, the material containing that information migrates from the reference collection to the general collection. Only infrequently will a reference work have so little intrinsic value that it shifts directly from the core of the library collection to the limbo of being totally withdrawn from the library.

GENERAL CRITERIA FOR WEEDING

For the general collection, the same criteria used for selecting materials should also be used in the weeding process. It is important to keep in mind that the library's collection is a reflection of the institution's or the community's educational, research, and recreational needs. Many libraries have collections of older materials that were acquired in unsystematic and inconsistent ways. A periodic review of the collection serves to weed these unused and inappropriate titles.[14]

The most commonly used criteria for weeding are use and age. Use is interpreted as the number of times per year that a title circulates, as well as the amount of time between transactions. Various studies have been done to establish the amount of time in which half of all of the uses of a title will occur. Circulation counts, shelf time patterns, in-library use, interlibrary loan requests, and citation analyses have all been used, either alone or in combination, to arrive at guidelines for retaining material in the collection.

Several other factors can also be used to select materials for potential weeding. In addition to usage, age is another fairly reliable predictor, especially in relation to the speed with which information becomes obsolete or inaccurate within a given subject field. For example, the period of depreciation for science and technology materials has been estimated at ten years, humanities fifteen years, and fiction five years.[15] The physical appearance of the material on the shelf can also be used. Removing materials that are damaged, old looking, printed on poor quality paper, or in need of repair will enhance the general appearance of the collection. Finally, subjective measures such as obsolete or misleading information, the librarian's knowledge of the field, opinions of reviewers or other experts, and the availability of the material in other libraries are also considered when establishing deselection guidelines.

The format of the material may also play some role in its evaluation for weeding purposes. Serials present special problems. It is more difficult to measure their usage because they often do not circulate outside of the library building. In-library use figures may have to be used, but these are unreliable measures of the use of a title because some patrons may reshelve the materials themselves. Instead of reviewing individual volumes, the entire set must be examined. Bostic[16] suggests determining the significance of a title by checking to see if it is included in standard indexing services, whether the title has ceased or the holdings are incomplete, and how often articles are cited. The three factors of usage, relevance, and availability elsewhere should be examined when determining the total worth of the journal.

CRITERIA FOR THE WEEDING
OF REFERENCE MATERIALS

When studying the reference collection, many of these criteria are not applicable. While space may occasionally prompt a weeding program, the relatively small space occupied by most reference collections is not generally a problem. Reference works usually do not circulate and their appearance is often irrelevant to their value as information sources. They also are not usually indexed by other sources, but are the indexes themselves. For reference works, the four criteria of usage, format, age, and comprehensiveness are the most important factors to be considered when evaluating material for weeding from the collection.

Applying the minimal growth model of reference collection development, the first criterion to be considered should be the use of the material. If a work is used constantly by the reference librarians, it should probably remain in the reference collection. If the usage level is low (as defined within that particular library), it should probably be transferred out of the reference collection. Reference librarians in different libraries will establish differing usage thresholds to determine inclusion in the reference collection. However, in almost any library, if a source is only used once a year or less, the patron using it may be better served by placing that material in the circulating collection rather than restricting it to the (presumably) noncirculating reference collection.

The second factor in reference evaluation is format. As mentioned above, reference works tend to be those that index or summarize knowledge presented in other places. The function of a reference work is to provide brief information quickly for the user. If a work does not effectively perform this function, it should be considered for weeding. Any source that requires an extended period of time for the user to retrieve the information will probably better serve the user in the circulating collection. Sources that at one time may have served as reference works for a given topic are often superseded by those that provide the same information in a more efficient or more timely manner.

Another important factor to consider in weeding is the currency of the information provided by the work. Sources that may at one time have been considered to be wonderful collections of useful material may be rendered virtually useless by the passage of time. Directories of people or organizations on a specific subject field are already out of date at the time of publication and usually become totally worthless for reference purposes after ten or more years. Even if no newer source has ever been published in the area, time may cause reference books to lose those intrinsic factors that enabled them to be considered reference works in the first place. It may be better for the library to provide no information on a topic than to provide incorrect and out-of-date material. Patrons seeking current information can be misled by outdated reference works.

Comprehensiveness is the final criterion to be examined when weeding reference materials. Some sources are replaced not by a newer work in the same area, but by one that covers the topic on a broader scope or provides a more in-depth treatment. This occurs frequently in fields that are rapidly changing, such as those discussing new technologies. Publishers will often latch on to new trends and try to produce handbooks or encyclopedias before a field has fully matured. When a solid research base has been established on the topic, a more complete reference work for the field is produced. Although only a short period of time may have passed between the two, the comprehensive nature of the second work will make it more desirable for patrons than the brief nature of the first.

When applying these criteria, the librarian must not look at each source in a vacuum, but must have a thorough knowledge of other reference sources in the same subject field. Weeding is a comparative process in which the various works on a given topic are examined as a group. Those that most efficiently and effectively index and/or summarize the topic will be kept in the reference collection. Those sources that are judged to be less useful as reference works will be transferred out. By comparing all works on a similar topic or of a similar type, the coverage of the collection will be kept internally consistent. When this occurs, the librarians and patrons alike will have a good expectation of which materials will be found in reference and which will be found in the general collection.

A SYSTEMATIC REFERENCE WEEDING PROGRAM

Almost every library in the world maintains a systematic selection process for its reference collection. Most libraries select and purchase new reference sources on a continuous basis as they become available. In order to maintain an effective reference collection, a systematic weeding process should also be conducted. As new materials are integrated into the collection, those outdated materials that they replace should be withdrawn. One procedure that may be followed in operating a systematic weeding program is that established by the Iowa State University Reference Department.

Most reference collections have an established weeding program, but may not even be aware that it exists. Titles for which the older editions are removed from the collection when the new edition is received comprise an automatic weeding process. In these cases, the weeding policy is established at the same time that the order for the new edition is placed. For serials, this weeding policy may be followed for many years without the input or knowledge of the librarians. Such automatic weeding of the reference collection serves to maintain an effective and usable collection for both the librarians and their patrons. This type of weeding policy should be encouraged whenever possible. However, most materials cannot be covered by such a system and must be handled on an individual basis. It is for this vast majority of reference works that a systematic weeding policy must be established.

The first step in the development of a systematic weeding project is to generate librarian support for such a program. Some reference librarians may fear that their favorite works will be taken away from them and sent to the general collection or, even worse, a storage location or withdrawn completely. In many cases, the librarians within the reference department will have differing philosophies of reference collection development. Before a program may begin, all of the librarians within the department must be made aware of the reasons for and goals of a weeding program. Once it is made clear that weeding will result in a better reference collection, then the program may begin.

A systematic weeding program should examine the entire reference collection on a regular basis. However, it is obvious that no one can evaluate the entire collection at one time. In order to provide continuous evaluation without overwhelming the staff, it is suggested that the librarians examine one subject area at a time. One of the most convenient methods for doing this is to begin with a broad call number section and proceed through that call number until the entire reference collection in that subject area has been evaluated. Dividing the collection into distinct call number segments, such as the 370s or the Ns, makes the weeding project manageable. A library may choose to weed the entire collection sequentially, beginning with the 000s or the As and proceeding to the end, or it may select call number sequences that are known to present problems. In either case, taking advantage of the natural subject breakdowns provided by the classification system establishes discrete and manageable units that can easily be evaluated.

The division of the collection into precise call number segments has other advantages as well. Most reference departments consisting of more than one person have established subject specializations among the various reference librarians. These subject divisions are usually intended to enable all of the librarians to participate in the selection process and to distribute the workload of reference collection development. The same subject expertise that is used in the selection of new materials may also be used in the evaluation of materials to be weeded from the collection. The involvement of subject specialists in the weeding project can help to raise the morale of the department by building on the concept that the reference collection is everyone's responsibility.

Unfortunately, not all of the input of subject specialists within the reference collection may be positive. If a subject specialist has a different philosophy of reference collection development than the majority of the staff, the criteria used for weeding may be vastly different if that person is selecting weeding materials. When one person weeds heavily and another lightly, the balance of the collection is in jeopardy. For this reason, the ISU program does not use subject specialists to select materials for weeding.

Under the Iowa State University plan, the Coordinator of Reference Collection Development selects items for review by the subject specialists. The subject specialist then reviews the material in question, along with any other interested reference librarians. In most cases, the librarians and subject specialists agree with the decisions of the Coordinator. When there is a disagreement, the Coordinator and the subject specialist confer about the specific title in question. As a result of that discussion, the specific work may either be withdrawn or retained within the reference collection. In either case, the evaluation and discussion of that title will have caused both the Coordinator and the subject specialist to thoroughly analyze the relevance of that work as a reference tool. The time spent on this process will reinforce the overall reference collection development philosophy of the department.

Under the ISU program, the Coordinator is expected to take a highly critical look at all materials in the reference collection. All sources not used frequently by the coordinator are examined for weeding. This critical approach is not done to develop an adversarial relationship between the Coordinator and the subject specialists, but to ensure that all works are equally considered for withdrawal. The Coordinator searches all works to determine if new editions have been published, if other works in the field have replaced the one under consideration, and to determine if the information in the work is still valid. By taking a critical approach to the weeding process, the Coordinator may be able to identify new materials to be added to the collection as well as older materials to be withdrawn.

Even when broken down by call number, the workload involved in such a program must be regulated so that it does not interfere with the other functions of the reference department or the other areas within the library, such as the technical services department. At Iowa State University, the Coordinator of Reference Collection Development selects one shelf of potential weeding books each week. While the Coordinator may need to study many shelves of books in the reference collection in order to arrive at one shelf of weeding candidates, each of the other librarians need only examine this one shelf. The Coordinator takes on the major workload of identifying potential weeding candidates, thus reducing the possible workload for the subject specialists. This amount of material also fits unobtrusively into the workload of the technical services department.

When a source is identified as one that is no longer needed in the reference collection, a decision must be reached on where it is to go. In most cases, the final location will be in the general circulating collection. However, other possibilities may include sending it to a branch library, a storage location, another department within the library, or completely withdrawing the item from the collection. If the reference librarians are also the subject bibliographers for the general collection, then the reference librarians may be able to make the final decision on the disposition of the item in question. In many libraries, the reference librarians have control over the reference collection, but someone from another department or division is responsible for developing the general collection. If this happens to be the case, it is important to have the other bibliographers involved in this decision. At Iowa State University, the appropriate subject bibliographers examine the materials that have been selected for weeding. While the reference librarians may make a recommendation as to the disposition of the item, the final decision is left to the subject bibliographer. This policy allows the bibliographer to have greater control over his or her collections and also serves to educate the bibliographer about the role of the reference collection within the entire library. The political benefits of such a program far outweigh the occasional change in disposition that a bibliographer may make over the reference librarians' suggestions.

After materials are selected and approved for removal from the reference collection, the process of transferring the item out of the collection must be completed. At Iowa State University, this process is conducted by a Library Assistant as a part of the regular workflow of that position. The transfer process can be quite time consuming, involving the updating of records, removal of catalog cards, filing of various forms, and the physical preparation of the volume. One of the primary reasons for conducting the weeding program at the rather slow pace of one shelf per week is to enable the paperwork to become a part of the normal workflow. For this reason, a slow and steady weeding program is often preferred over a crash weeding project by the technical services personnel and other support staff.

CONCLUSION

The weeding of the reference collection is necessary in order to maintain a current and useful reference collection. Reference weeding will help both the librarians and the users find those materials that most effectively index and summarize the information contained in the rest of the library. A systematic weeding program such as that used at Iowa State University allows the librarians to continually evaluate the materials contained in the reference collection without creating an overwhelming additional workload. Since most materials removed from the reference collection are transferred to another location within the library and are not totally withdrawn from the collection, the problem of weeding materials that may later be requested by patrons is solved. If a mistake in weeding is made, it is usually correctable. While it may take some efforts to promote a systematic weeding program to other librarians and to the public, such a program should eliminate the problem that Jim Rettig terms a "bibliographic Love Canal."[17] We encourage other libraries to adopt a similar program and to aggressively weed their reference collections. For most reference collections, more is not necessarily better.

REFERENCES

1. Evans, G. Edward. *Developing Library and Information Center Collections*, 2d ed. Littleton, CO, Libraries Unlimited, 1987, pp. 291-309.

2. Mosher, Paul H. "Managing Library Collections: The Process of Review and Pruning" in *Collection Development in Libraries: A Treatise*, Robert D. Stueart and George B. Miller, eds. Greenwich, CT, JAI Press, 1980, pp. 164-166.

3. Slote, Stanley J. *Weeding Library Collections – II*, 2nd rev. ed. Littleton, CO, Libraries Unlimited, 1982, p. 43.

4. Lucker, Jay K., Kate S. Herzog, and Sydney J. Owens. "Weeding Collections in an Academic Library System: Massachusetts Institute of Technology." *Science and Technology Libraries*, 6(3), 1986, p. 13.

5. Lancaster, F. W. "Obsolescence, Weeding, and the Utilization of Space" in *If You Want to Evaluate Your Library . . .*, Champaign, IL, University of Illinois Graduate School of Library and Information Science, 1988, p. 77.

6. Slote, Stanley J. op. cit. pp. 20-22. Also Segal, Joseph P. *Evaluating and Weeding Collections in Small and Medium-Sized Public Libraries: The CREW Method*, Chicago, American Library Association, 1980, pp. 19-20.

7. Nichols, Margaret Irby. "Weeding the Reference Collection." *Texas Library Journal*, 62(1), 1986, pp. 204-206.

8. Westbrook, Lynn. "Weeding Reference Serials." *Serials Librarian*, 10(4), 1986, pp. 81-100.

9. Engeldinger, Eugene A. "Weeding of Academic Library Reference Collections: A Survey of Current Practice." *RQ*, 25(3), 1986, pp. 367-371.

10. Biggs, Mary and Victor Biggs. "Reference Collection Development in Academic Libraries: Report of a Survey." *RQ*, 27(1), 1987, pp. 71-74.

11. Rettig, James. "Love Canal in the Reference Stacks." *Reference Services Review*, 10(4), 1982, p. 7. Also Schlachter, Gail. "Obsolescence, Weeding, and Bibliographic Love Canals." *RQ*, 28(1), 1988, pp. 7-8.

12. Schlachter, Gail. ibid.

13. This has been the basis for several discussions at the "Heads of Reference of Medium-Sized Academic Libraries Discussion Group" at the annual and midwinter conferences of the American Library Association.

14. Mosher, Paul H. op. cit.

15. Lancaster, F. W. op. cit. pp. 72-76.

16. Bostic, Mary J. "Serials Deselection." *Serials Librarian*, 9(3), 1985, pp. 86-89.

17. Rettig, James. op. cit.

Let's Get Rid of It:
A Reference Librarian's Battle Cry

Steven F. Vincent

SUMMARY. A recent survey revealed that very few libraries were doing any significant weeding in their reference collections. Yet weeding the reference collection may have as great an impact on the library as a whole as weeding the general collection. This article discusses some of the author's experiences weeding the reference collection at Georgia State University and the ways in which general weeding concerns, such as planning for staffing, establishing criteria, and formulating selection policies, may be applied to the reference collection. Reference materials differ in nature and use from materials in the general collection, and this article analyses the impact these differences have on the weeding effort.

Weeding is generally regarded as a thankless task. In fact, it may be less troublesome to build a new library or library annex than to weed a library's collections. Nevertheless, there has been a great deal of interest in weeding in the library literature of late; however, with the exception of a recent survey by Eugene Engeldinger,[1] there has been little attention given to the problems of weeding reference collections. In the definitive work on weeding, Stanley Slote made only a passing reference to the reference collection, saying only that "depending upon the level of reference services it is called upon to perform, no weeding should be done except for replacing certain works with newer editions or more definitive works."[2]

Quite a few years ago, the reference staff at Georgia State University realized that, unless some weeding were done in the reference collection, the clutter in the reference stacks would have a

---

Steven F. Vincent is Librarian, Boyd Lee Spahr Library, Dickinson College, Carlisle, PA 17013.

serious impact on "the level of services it is called upon to perform." The number of stack ranges had increased by more than fifty percent, yet new volumes still could not be properly shelved; books were packed so tightly that many were damaged and a great deal of time was spent searching for volumes that had become wedged behind others on the shelves. A new library annex was on the way, but it would not be completed for nearly eight years, and when completed, the reference collection was to remain in its present location with no additional space expected. Some of the more sensitive members of the department were subject to fits of sneezing when retrieving volumes from the shelves, leading many to suspect that quite a few volumes could be assigned to less accessible storage with no loss of service. It is germane to point out, however, that there already was a weeding program in place: each librarian was assigned a section of shelves to shelf-read, with instructions to pull damaged, outdated, or otherwise unusable volumes. Fully a quarter of the staff found time to prune their assigned ranges at least once a year, yielding an annual harvest of about fifty weeds.

A number of possible courses of action were explored and rejected: it was felt that a fire-sale would give librarians too little say in what remained in the collection; shaking the shelves and letting the ripe books fall would raise too great a dust cloud and might injure someone browsing the lower shelves; and Agent Orange was rejected as too dangerous. Therefore, the Institutional Approach was deemed best: we formed a committee. The committee met and reached the unanimous consensus that no one had the slightest idea how to proceed; some members had found time to examine the first edition of Slote's book,[3] while others had done some literature searching. No one had found a single article on weeding reference collections or on the use of reference materials. A 1978 bibliography on weeding in academic libraries by Barbara Rice identified nothing dealing with reference collections.[4] An online search of ERIC using the keywords "weeding" and "reference books" turned up nothing except a bibliography on gardening. This informational void seems to sum up current practice in weeding reference collections. In Engeldinger's survey, about twenty percent of the reference librarians responded that they do no weeding at all. Of those who do weed, two-thirds reported that they weed fewer than one hundred volumes per year.[5]

WHY WEED REFERENCE?

Members of this committee, dubbed the Ad Hoc committee On the Reference Collection (AHORC), were as concerned with the Why of weeding as the How. After a little reflection, it seems clear that many of the reasons most often given for weeding general collections may be as valid for the reference collection. As Robert Stueart, in a concise overview of weeding, stated, "one must evaluate materials before purchasing them, and . . . re-evaluate their usefulness to the collection and then remove them, if they have lost their value."[6] Weeding should be seen as a positive activity in enhancing the collection, as necessary to maintaining a healthy reference collection as housecleaning. The late Jesse Shera phrased it a little more strongly: "Someone, now unhappily forgotten, has said that he was alarmed by the growth of two things in our society — libraries and cemeteries — and proposed cremation as the solution to both."[7]

Even in the planning stages, there are some benefits which may be realized. Jutta Reed-Scott outlined the steps in planning a weeding project as: (1) analyze why the collection needs to be weeded, (2) analyze options such as discarding materials, removing lesser used materials to off-site storage, and replacing materials with microforms or other formats, and (3) determine how much it is feasible to accomplish given time and staffing constraints.[8] Therefore, the planning stage of a weeding project may lead to an analysis of staffing priorities and areas of the collection in need of weeding or development.

If the elimination of out-dated materials, the removal of physically deteriorated or damaged materials which will not withstand heavy use, and making room for newer works or works on more currently popular or significant topics are major concerns in weeding the general collection, why should they not be considered in maintaining the reference collection? Reference collections are even more subject to space constraints than general collections, since they are usually confined to a single floor — or a portion of a single floor. It is impossible to continue to add shelving to the reference stacks indefinitely.

Reference collections must keep pace with new areas of research or shifts in the goals or programs of their parent institutions, just as do the general collections. Colleges and universities are continually updating their curricula, adding new programs and deleting others. New reference works must be added to support new areas of study, while reference tools which no longer support the curriculum ought to be removed. Reference books age as quickly as the books in the general collection do—perhaps more quickly; old bibliographies and encyclopedias no longer accurately reflect the state of current research in their subject areas. Weeding should be seen as a responsibility to the institution.

If time permits, the weeding project may be an ideal time for collection building. As volumes are considered for removal one may investigate the availability of newer editions or more comprehensive works. It will give librarians an opportunity to learn what is in the collection and bolster subject areas which are somewhat weak. Unfortunately, this places an even greater burden on the staffing.

DISPOSING OF WEEDS

As Slote has suggested, not every weeded book needs to be destroyed or removed from the library, but many may be removed from the primary stacks or most heavily used portions of the collection.[9] This is particularly relevant for reference works, since by "weeding" we may simply mean moving them to the circulating collection or "research" stacks. In fact, the usefulness of some volumes in the reference collection may be enhanced by allowing them to circulate. Large urban institutions with widely scattered populations, such as regional libraries or universities with large commuter student bodies, may find that allowing lesser-used materials to circulate will allow patrons to make much better use of them.

The unique nature of reference materials should also be taken into consideration when weeding them. Reference books may be viewed as access tools, rather than as primary or secondary information sources. Their function is to unlock the holdings of the rest of the library, to introduce a subject matter and provide a strategy for researching it, and to provide brief identifications or directory information within the subject areas supported by the collection. Therefore, it is often possible to discard reference books without losing information.

Weeding and collection development should ideally go hand-in-hand. This is one of the advantages of weeding which often is overlooked. As one contemplates the disposal of a dated reference book, one should also consider identifying a newer bibliography which includes references to more current research, or a newer handbook or encyclopedia which provides a more accurate or complete summation of the knowledge in its subject area.

OBSTACLES TO WEEDING

Next AHORC turned its attention to the obstacles which it would have to overcome. By its second meeting, the members of the committee were well aware of the greatest of these: the meeting had to be scheduled around hours manning the desk, filing services, and performing computer searches. In spite of the fact that the committee's work was to be regarded as a major project, the routine duties of a reference department do not allow a great deal of flexibility in scheduling other activities, so weeding was to be assigned a fairly low priority. Recognizing the enormous responsibilities borne by their colleagues, AHORC saw its major responsibility would be to maximize the efforts of the weeders.

Weeding may be approached in two ways from a staffing standpoint: it may be designated a routine maintenance duty, engaged in on a daily basis by all or a designated group of librarians, or as a crash project, with some or all librarians assigned to it on a more or less full-time basis. Danny Bedsole has suggested that systematic weeding spreads the work load and maintains an up-to-date collection, but day-to-day pressures make it difficult to fit daily weeding into the usual routine.[10] This has been the past experience at GSU. A crash project may enable the librarians to view the collection as a whole, gaining insight into its strengths and weaknesses, but, as Bedsole pointed out, it may not be possible to free staff members from other duties for a concerted weeding effort.[11]

A tersely worded note from the Catalog Department apprised AHORC that there may be another potential problem. The exact wording of the note has been lost, but this is a rough paraphrase:

> If you wish us to cease processing new books, abandon converting records to machine-readable format for use in COM and online catalogs, halt repairing labels and damaged books, and visit our families only every other weekend in order to effect reference book transfers in a timely and courteous manner, we respectfully suggest that you . . .

A similar note was forthcoming from the Circulation Department, concerning the placement of transferred volumes in already overcrowded stacks. Rare is that library where technical and public service units are on such friendly terms that weeding the reference collection will be given priority by other departments.

Other library departments are not the only groups which need to be won over to a weeding project, however. Patrons, faculty, even one's own colleagues in the Reference Department may raise objections. Reference librarians are subject to an occupational disease which other library staff do not generally suffer from. Known as "Preferred Book Syndrome," it is usually more pronounced among more experienced reference librarians, although it may infect even the youngest. Its principal symptom is a dread of parting with a reference tool relied upon successfully in the past, even though it may have become outdated or have been replaced by newer or more comprehensive works. Reference librarians also frequently suffer from an unnatural dread of making a mistake: since many lack expertise in subject areas, they feel that they can't accurately judge the value of items they consider for discard. Jesse Shera suggested that the library's clientele may be better served by placing persons with subject competencies, who understand books as sources of information rather than as physical objects to be processed, stored and retrieved, in charge of the acquisition, organization, retrieval, and eventual disposal of library materials.[12] An alternative is to employ non-library faculty and subject-specialists as weeders and selectors, but the interests of faculty and subject specialists are usually too narrowly focused to view the collection as a whole.

The fact is that librarians are somewhat afraid of weeding, of putting their knowledge of the collection—or lack thereof—on the line and exposing it to criticism from the outside. Shera summed it up best: "Librarians are so afraid of being considered censors that they almost reach a point where they have no selection policy, certainly no rejection policy or elimination policy and this has hampered us."[13] Perhaps, rather than designating them "selection" policies, we should call them rejection policies; by this I mean, of all the excellent publications available, what is the rationale for not adding some of them to the collection. If collection development were viewed in this light, weeding would be much simpler to justify to the library's patrons and to the librarians themselves.

PROBLEMS WITH PATRONS

Patrons and faculty generally don't recognize the importance of weeding. Some faculty members tend to view the reference collection as an extension of the reserve reading room and regularly assign readings from a favorite handbook. This causes problems not only for weeders, but for those charged with keeping reference materials on the shelves, since this handbook is the first item to disappear at the peak of the semester rush. At state-supported institutions, public-spirited taxpayers, perhaps even legislators, may question the discarding of state-owned property.

But the major patron-related problem in weeding a reference collection is that we usually don't know who the patrons are. As at GSU, reference collections are usually more accessible to users unaffiliated with the institution than the general collection. Circulation departments usually require some kind of valid user's card, while often special collection areas, sometimes even general stacks, are closed to those without valid identification. But reference departments are usually expected to serve anyone who can find the library's entrance.

What materials the reference department's users, affiliated or not, are using is also a mystery. While circulation statistics may be useful as a guide in weeding the circulating portions of the collection, the only statistics kept at the reference desk are the numbers of questions asked. As stated above, no one has done a study of how reference materials are used. AHORC attempted a brief study: for a short period, student shelvers were asked to count the number of books reshelved in each of the LC classifications. A study of the results indicated that we were shelving a lot of books, but there was no apparent correlation between books shelved and books to be weeded.

William McGrath made a study to determine if there is a correlation between in-house and out-house (if that is the term) use of library materials. By tallying the subject areas of books found lying on tables and comparing them with circulation statistics, he found a rough correlation between the subjects of books circulated and those used in-house.[14] Lawrence and Oja confirmed that there is a weak correlation between in-house and out-house use at Berkeley.[15] They found that there were roughly six "unrecorded" uses (i.e., in-house) for every use recorded in circulation statistics,[16] so that we may surmise that reference collections are more heavily used than circulating collections. What all this points to is that the reference collection ought to be strong in those areas in which the library circulates the most materials; this is the equivalent to saying that the reference collection should meet its mission of supporting the role of the parent institution.

The impact of all this on weeding criteria is even less clear when we recognize that it is fairly well established that use patterns vary in different academic disciplines, so that use criteria may not be equally applicable in all subject areas. For example, should we apply the same weeding criteria in Icelandic literature that we do in medicine? Lawrence and Oja also reported differences in use rates between types of materials distinguished by characteristics such as circulation history and form of publication, as well as subject area,[17] so one may infer that the use patterns of the non-circulating reference collection will also vary somewhat from those of the general collection.

So, the bottom line is that the reference collection should contain all that it is appropriate for it to contain, the subjects represented should be the subjects of interest to the library of which it is a part. But is there an ideal size for a reference collection? Is 30,000 volumes adequate for a large, research library, or is 20,000 enough? According to Slote, "large, heavily used reference collections . . . should satisfy at least 99.5 to 100 percent of the anticipated use,"[18] but how does one anticipate the use of a reference collection? This is the heart of the problem, we don't know how to evaluate the quality of collections; we can easily measure the size of collections, how frequently books circulate, and how many books circulate; and the natural assumption is that the bigger the number, the better the collection.

HOW TO PROCEED

So, finding little help in the literature of librarianship and faced with the task of blazing a new trail through some very tall weeds, AHORC quickly identified areas of concern for a weeding project: criteria for deselecting materials, what to do with weeded materials, where to find the time and enough warm bodies to do the work, and just how to proceed with it.

To establish weeding criteria, the committee turned to the department's book selection policy. This policy had been in effect for a couple of years, and at the time of its adoption, it was intended that weeding would be an on-going process. Therefore, it included some general guidelines on weeding, which were summarized in the statement: "Would this publication be placed in Reference according to the selection criteria if it came through on the new book truck?" AHORC examined these guidelines and made some modifications to better address the problems it faced. Frequency of use was the first criterion mentioned, but it was also agreed that it would not be the only consideration; also mentioned were age and condition of the volume; its research value, regardless of use; and the extent of the coverage of the subject in the collection. Stueart has enumerated some other possible considerations: length of time since its last circulation (not necessarily applicable to reference collections), availability of multiple copies, language of material, availability of material elsewhere, through interlibrary loan or local consortia, and coverage in indexes and bibliographies and frequency of citation.[19]

The book selection policy is invaluable in the weeding process. As Bedsole indicated, a selection policy based on the aims and objectives of the institution is the key not only to weeding, but to collection maintenance.[20] The Reference Book Selection Policy at GSU identifies types of materials, including how many years of almanacs and yearbooks, which are to be included in the collection and delineates subjects of interest to the collection. The committee reviewed these guidelines and made a few modifications for the task at hand. Such a policy aided the individual weeders in their evaluations of weeding candidates and provided an instrument to show faculty and interested patrons that the decisions of the weeders were not capricious. The GSU Reference Book Selection Policy does not specify a size for the collection, although the latest revision includes the following statement:

> There is no designated limit on the size of the reference collection. However, changes in the curriculum and research interests of faculty, and availability of and need for additional resources in various disciplines shall serve as guidelines to the relative growth rates of subject areas within the collection. It must also be borne in mind that, although there is no predetermined ideal size for the collection, there are definite physical limitations on the amount of space available to house the collection. Therefore, development of the collection must go hand-in-hand with an active weeding program to assure the availability of the best possible collection within the space constraints.

However, of late I have had second thoughts on this point. It may be better to set an optimum size for a reference collection, even for a whole library. As Shera said, "The time's rapidly approaching, I think, when we are going to have to think of libraries as not growing continually, but growing by replacement."[21] Given the space constraints of the typical reference collection, I think it may be preferable for each library to set a size for the reference collection, 15,000 volumes, for example, and charge the reference librarian with maintaining the most appropriate 15,000 volumes for the institution.

IMPACT ON THE USE OF THE COLLECTION

Reflecting on weeding criteria brought about a reevaluation of the function of the books in the reference collection. The selection policy indicated that the reference collection was intended to support the curriculum and general reference service, but the nature of that support was undefined. It was decided certain types of reference works which did not require the assistance of a librarian for their use, such as specialized bibliographies on graduate-level subjects, could be placed in the circulating collection, while other types of materials intended for a specialized audience, business-related loose-leaf services, for example, might be placed in a non-circulating category in the general collection.

To assure the integrity of the general collection and to avoid unnecessary duplication, all reference department weeding decisions were forwarded to the Chief Bibliographer, who might decide to discard an item that would be duplicated in the general collection or to retain in the general collection something that, in his judgement, may have value. Since removal from the reference collection does not automatically mean removal from the library, in many respects weeding decisions in the reference collection are easier to make than in the general collection.

If all aspects of the weeding project had been this easy, AHORC may even have enjoyed its task. Quite early on, however, it became apparent that the reference librarians could go through the collection much more quickly than the catalogers could remove the deselected items. In fact, some books were weeded twice before the catalogers could pick them up, with a different disposition requested the second time. (Catalogers tend to be of an orderly frame of mind; they find this kind of inconsistency upsetting.) So AHORC felt it necessary to find separate storage for deselected items, in order to avoid unnecessary duplication of effort and confusion. Since one of the aims of weeding was to free space for new materials, this option was preferred to targeting the weeded items in some way and returning them to their regular shelves. This issue of temporary storage was one that had not occurred to AHORC in the planning phases, and it made the early stages of the weeding project more difficult.

STAFFING

Finding time and warm bodies proved to be the most difficult part of the project, however. To illustrate this, I quote from the archives of the committee: AHORC ". . . recommends that the Reference Department undertake an extensive weeding of the Reference Collection beginning during the August quarter break. The anticipated completion date for the project is December 31." The August break and December date alluded to were both in the year 1981. A 1989 communication from my former colleagues at Georgia State indicated that they were nearing the end of the weeding project. Planning for time and personnel will always be the most difficult aspect of weeding.

As I have attempted to show, weeding is hard. It is much easier to add more space than it is to prune a collection. In many respects, our job is much harder than the surgeon's, because it is so difficult for us to see books as diseased tissue. But I think it will become more and more necessary for us to cut healthy tissue, that is, books which have some value, to insure the health of our collections, for it will not always be possible to add more and more storage. Reference collections, with their greater space constraints may be the first areas to feel this. Jesse Shera, again, has put it so well:

> I think the day is going to come when the problem for the librarian will not be book acquisition but book elimination. This is a far more difficult job because it is always easy once you get a book to keep it—oh, it is there, it's not doing any harm, let it stay, it's difficult to say this stuff is no longer valid.

Let's get rid of it.[22]

REFERENCES

1. Eugene A. Engeldinger, "Weeding of Academic Library Reference Collections: a Survey of Current Practice," *RQ* (Spring 1986), 366-371.

2. Stanley J. Slote, *Weeding Library Collections—II* (2d. rev. ed.; Littleton, CO: Libraries Unlimited, 1982), p. 55-56.

3. Stanley J. Slote, *Weeding Library Collections* (Littleton, CO: Libraries Unlimited, 1975).

4. Barbara A. Rice, "Weeding in Academic and Research Libraries: an Annotated Bibliography," *Collection Management*, II (Spring 1978), 65-71.

5. Engeldinger, "Weeding of Academic Library Reference Collections," 368.

6. Robert D. Stueart, "Weeding of Library Materials—Politics and Policies," *Collection Management* VII (Summer 1985), 49.

7. Jesse H. Shera, "The Up-Side-Down Library," *Utah Libraries* (Spring 1978), 15.

8. Jutta Reed-Scott, "Implementation of a Weeding Program," *Collection Management* VII (Summer 1985), 60.

9. Slote, *Weeding Library Collections—II*, p. 14.

10. Danny T. Bedsole, "Formulating a Weeding Policy for Books in a Special Library," *Special Libraries* XLIX (May-June 1958), 206-207.

11. Ibid.

12. Shera, "The Up-Side-Down Library," p. 17.

13. Shera, "The Up-Side-Down Library," p. 15.

14. William E. McGrath, "Correlating the Subjects of Books Taken Out of and Books Used Within an Open-Stack Library," *College and Research Libraries* XXXII (July 1971), 280-285.

15. Gary S. Lawrence and Anne R. Oja, *The Use of General Collections at the University of California* (Berkeley: University of California Systemwide Administration, 1980), p. 59.

16. Lawrence and Oja, *Use of General Collections*, p. vi.

17. Lawrence and Oja, *Use of General Collections*, p. ix.

18. Slote, *Weeding Library Collections—II*, p. 56.

19. Stueart, "Weeding of Library Materials," p. 52-53.

20. Bedsole, "Formulating a Weeding Policy," p. 206.

21. Shera, "The Up-Side-Down Library," p. 14.

22. Shera, "The Up-Side-Down Library," p. 14.

Managing the Reference Collection: The Practice of Pruning

Bart Harloe
Helen M. Barber

SUMMARY. This essay presents the case for pruning an academic reference collection. Rather than a theoretical discourse on the virtues and vices of weeding, we present a practical discussion that focuses on the actual implementation of a reference pruning project. Thus we cover the planning stages, the logistics of organization, criteria for weeding, and the communication issues that seem always to arise during a weeding project. We also discuss various modes and modalities for dealing with conflict resolution as well as the vexing question of how to deal with reference serials in both their traditional and electronic formats. The emphasis throughout the paper is on the practical problems, issues, and concerns likely to confront librarians attempting to organize and carry out a reference collection review/pruning program.

Without a rational, objective, and systematic approach to collection management, how can we be confident that our sources are current and relevant? Without up-to-date sources, how can we possibly provide accurate reference service?[1]

Gail Schlacter, *RQ*, Fall 1988

INTRODUCTION

This essay is written from the point of a practicing librarian. Thus, the discussion will not be theoretical, and no extensive bibli-

Bart Harloe was Head, Collection Management, New Mexico State University Library, when this paper was written. He is currently Assistant Director, Collection Development and Management, Honnold Library, Claremont College, Claremont, CA 91711. Helen M. Barber is Reference Librarian and Reference Collection Development Coordinator, New Mexico State University Library, Box 30006, Las Cruces, NM 88003-0006.

ography will be provided. It is for those who intend to tackle a reference collection, review it, prune it, and otherwise engage in an active program of reference collection management. The focus is on the academic library situation, but it is hoped that many of the principles, practices, and examples elucidated here will be relevant to other reference contexts, whether it be in a public or special library.

WHY DO IT?

For the reference librarian, burdened with the usual set of responsibilities — i.e., reference work, online searching, bibliographic instruction sessions, and academic committees, the question does come up: Why do it? It is time-consuming, dusty, and at times frustrating work. There are probably many good reasons for regularly pruning the reference collection, but we would like to emphasize two here: (1) such a practice conducted on a regular basis will provide for an up-to-date reference collection that is more likely to provide accurate answers to the questions put to us by our patrons; and (2) a regularly pruned reference collection is more likely to be a real working collection, rather than an historical accretion of reference sources. A leaner, more utilitarian collection will also prove to be more accessible and useful to the reference librarians themselves, especially to those new members of the reference department who need to be trained and oriented to the strengths and weaknesses of the collection.

What are the disadvantages? As mentioned above, the work is time-consuming and dusty. Perhaps even more importantly, there is likely to be conflict involved in such work, because "weeding" seems to be fraught with difficulties (from both an organizational and an emotional point of view).

ORGANIZING THE EFFORT

Collection Policy Statements

Arguments pro and con have been made with regard to the value of a written collection development policy statement. We will not rehearse those arguments here but rather refer to the fact that if you do not already have a collection policy statement, the process of pruning a reference collection is likely to lead you quickly to the conclusion that such a policy is essential to handle the questions that will come up as a matter of course. For example, how do we handle almanacs? What are the criteria for currency, insofar as reference serials are concerned? What about bibliographies in the reference collection? When you approach the reference collection with the intention of reviewing for the purpose of pruning outdated material, the utility of a policy statement covering different formats will become readily apparent.

We would further argue that a specific policy for weeding should also be in place as one proceeds to weed the collection. Now obviously, there are two ways to go about creating such policies, if they do not already exist. One is to take the time to develop and ratify such statements *before* beginning the actual collection review. The other approach is to improvise and create policies to cover specific cases as you go along with the actual collection review. If time permits, the former option is probably to be preferred. Some issues will require more time for resolution than others, and it is probably best to resolve as many of the macro-level policy issues before getting into the "nitty-gritty" collection review process itself. This is the ideal approach, but we all know that circumstances are seldom ideal. In fact, circumstances seem always to conspire against a "rational" approach to such problems.

Perhaps there is some comfort to be gained from the fact that the *process* of creating such policy statements can be very valuable in and of itself, regardless of the real outcome in terms of documentation. It is probably also true that the group will not only learn much from the discussion of basic principles but that the attempt to *apply* such general principles will also be fruitful to the collective understanding of the strengths and weaknesses of the reference collection.

Now let us assume that the question of policy statements has been resolved to the satisfaction of parties involved. How do we go about planning the weeding of a reference collection? A good point of departure for such planning might be the following suggestions made by Paul Mosher:[2]

1. Determine how much staff time will be needed, and how much may reasonably be demanded, not only from collection development, but also from acquisitions, circulation, and cataloging.
2. Write procedures and design the necessary forms.
3. Develop a timetable for the project based on the staff time and the space required for different phases.
4. Inform participating staff of the project's goals and procedures, the specific assignments to be made, and the timetable for the project.
5. Obtain faculty input on the plan itself and on the disposition of weeded materials.

The above strictures should in general apply to all collections, but other unique questions need to be addressed when the collection that is to be weeded/reviewed is composed of reference materials. For example, who is to be involved? Reference libarians, all library selectors, teaching faculty? In terms of the division of labor with the collection review program for reference, who decides on which subject areas? Who is responsible for the secondary review? Who has the final say and how is that decision to be reached? If there are differences of opinion, how are those differences to be resolved? A process for resolving conflicts needs to be established at the outset, so that when the time comes to deal with conflict, everyone understands the "rules of the game."

Communication with Technical Services

Before a library undertakes to prune the reference collection, the division of labor between public and technical service staff needs to be made very clear. Everyone involved in the process should understand who is responsible for deselection and who is responsible for processing the deselected items. Communication with technical services staff needs to be consistent, constant, and current. In fact, this aspect of the process is so important to the successful outcome of a weeding project that the library may want to consider providing a coordinating committee to deal with the technical questions relating to weeding the reference collection.

Reference Serials

One question that will surely occupy a great deal of everyone's time is the question of how to deal with reference serials. In this age of radical price increases, the proliferation of electronic reference sources in serial form, and the consequent need to cancel serials, nothing is more important than the development of a coherent approach to this issue. The policy statements described above will need to include a section that outlines the library's approach to reference serials. In terms of the actual pruning of the collection, questions concerning cut-dates and cancellations will quickly arise. What should be withdrawn? What should be sent to the general collection? What should be the general rule on cut-dates for reference serials? What about the cancellation of serials titles that appear to duplicate material provided elsewhere in the library? Are there CD-ROM products that might be substituted for their print versions? The reference department will quickly find that questions such as these will consume a great deal of time. Insofar as possible, these questions should be dealt with at the policy level *before* beginning the actual pruning. Later in this essay we will return to the question of reference serials.

IMPLEMENTATION: COORDINATING THE PROJECT

Before describing the implementation of a pruning project, let us reiterate some of the planning assumptions cited above:

1. You will need some policy guidelines, so allow time for the development of such guidelines *before* the actual implementation of the project, if possible.

2. Make sure that there is a clear understanding of the division of labor between public and technical services staff with regard to the deselection and processing of materials.

3. Make sure that everyone involved understands the structure and the process of decision-making for the project. If the final decisions on matters of procedures/policy are to be made by a coordinating group, then provision needs to be made for regular meetings of that group. If the question "who's in charge here?" keeps coming

up, then you know that the coordinating group has not properly
done its job.

4. Finally, in carrying out such a project, it is important to allow
enough time to complete the various phases of the project, extend-
ing from policy formation and planning to deselection and processing. While it is essential to have an action plan, it is also important
to be flexible within the schedule presented by that plan. Some time
will also be needed for the resolution of conflicts that will inevitably
arise in this sort of process. We will return to this topic later.

Types of Material to Be Reviewed and Criteria for Pruning

A useful procedure for a project of this kind is to utilize review
slips (see Figures 1-3). The review slips can be inserted in the book
and left for a specific period of time for review. Before actual use,
the decision slips should be reviewed by reference *and* technical
services staff to ensure that the information asked for on the slip is
appropriate. It is important that reviewers fill out the forms as completely as possible and check the criteria for decision making. In
terms of the criteria for weeding, the following three categories will
probably cover 90% of the material that you will be reviewing:

1. *Weeding for Discard* (see Figure 1): Use this slip for material
   that appears to be outdated and/or superseded.

You will probably be surprised at how much of this type of material you will find in your reference collection, especially if this is
the *first* time that you have made a concerted effort to review your
collection. Oftentimes, a book is simply too problematic from a
physical point of view to keep in the collection. However, if the
information contained in the book is considered to be current and/or
useful, consider ordering a replacement title.

What criteria should be applied at this stage of the process?
Kathleen Coleman and Pauline Dickinson are correct when they
argue that "it is impossible to establish absolute standards to be
followed in weeding. For some disciplines the reference collection
should provide current material only; for others it must also provide
retrospective and historical works."[3] However, we share with these

Date: _____
Reviewer's Initials: _____
Department: _____

Reference Collection WITHDRAWAL Slip

(Please Print)

Call No.: _____

Author: _____

Title: _____

_____

No. of vol(s) on shelf: _____

No. of copies on shelf: _____

This title has been identified as a candidate for withdrawal. The reason for withdrawal is checked below:

☐ Duplicate title

☐ Outdated or
Superceded edition

☐ Physical condition of
volume

☐ Other (Please state):

If you disagree with the above decision, sign your name and state your reason(s) for disagreement:

Name: _____

Dept: _____

Reason for disagreement: _____
_____
_____
_____

Disagreement resolved: _____

Date: _____

Tech. Services Action Completed: _____

Date: _____

(Figure 1)

two authors the belief that these "general criteria" are appropriate in approaching a reference weeding project: "(1) Significance of the publication; (2) Age and currency of the publication; (3) Availability of later editions; (4) Physical condition of the publication; (5) Duplication of the contents in more recent works; (6) Language of the publication."[4]

2. *Review for Relocation* (Figure 2): You may want to slip titles that you believe should be kept in the library's collection, but not necessarily in the reference collection.

Remember that a primary criterion for a reference title is that it ought to be a "working" title which is consulted on a fairly regular basis. The definition of what constitutes a working title will, of course, vary from institution to institution, but your policy statement should at least make an attempt to define what the phrase "working reference collection" means for you.

3. *Reference Serials* (Figure 3): Continuations will present a special series of difficulties for those involved in a review of a reference collection.

First, guidelines for cut-dates must be established. If you decide to keep a title in reference, how complete a run do you need in your working collection? Decision rules will need to be established because from a processing point of view it will be very difficult to make unique decisions on each title. For example, will the library keep two years in reference and then discard? Will the library keep two years in reference, then five years in the circulating collection, and then discard? While the options are not limitless, the library will need to develop consistent guidelines that allow it to treat most of its reference serials in a rational fashion.

Second, there is the question of reducing overlap and duplication amongst reference serials. This is an especially vexing question in the age of electronic information sources. The budget impacts of such decisions are also very important. Reference serials tend to be expensive. The library should use this opportunity to review its reference serials and eliminate those serials that appear to duplicate or overlap with other sources. The following helpful hints that might

Date: _____
Reviewer's Initials: _____
Department: _____

Reference Collection RELOCATION Slip

Call No.: _____
Author: _____
Title: _____
             _____

This title is a candidate to be sent
to the Circulating Collection, for
the reasons checked below:

☐ Should be available for
  circulation.

☐ Not a working reference
  title.

☐ Too specialized or narrow
  a focus to be useful in
  Reference.

☐ Other

If you disagree with this decision,
sign your name and state your reason
for disagreement:

Name: _____

Dept: _____

Reason for disagreement: _____
_____
_____
_____

(Figure 2)

Date: _____
Reviewer's Initials: _____
Department _____

Reference Serials Review Slip

Call No.: _____
Author: _____
Title: _____

Processing Decision for Reference SERIALS

Reference Serials require a decision
as to cut-date. Recommend that this
title be treated as follows:

☐ Keep entire run in
Reference

☐ Keep 2 yrs. in Reference,
then weed from library
collection.

☐ Keep 2 yrs. in Reference,
5 yrs. in general collection,
then weed from library collection.

☐ Keep 2 yrs. in Reference,
entire back-run in General
collection.

☐ Other: _____

_____

_____

If you disagree with the above decision,
sign your name and state your reason(s)
for disagreement:

Name: _____
Dept: _____
Reason for disagreement: _____

_____

_____

_____

(Figure 3)

further your efforts in this area have been suggested by David Tyckoson:[5]

1. *Cancel duplicate subscriptions.* This will save space and money — though it also decreases access to popular sources while keeping those used infrequently. (Tyckoson's examples include *World Almanac* and *Statistical Abstract.*)

2. *Substitute older editions for some current subscriptions.* Where duplicates are housed in different locations, the latest edition might be kept in reference and the previous edition used elsewhere. (Tyckoson's examples include *Books in Print* and *British Books in Print.*)

3. *Cancel services updating frequently published works.* Some such supplements may be too expensive for the information provided and the use received — especially if the information is available online. (Tyckoson's examples include *New Associations* and *New Trade Names.*)

4. *Subscribe only to annual cumulations of some indexes.* Where searches of other sources may substitute, or where information is available online, the annual cumulation of less frequently used indexes may suffice. (Tyckoson's examples include *Astronomy and Astrophysics Abstracts* and *PAIS Foreign Language Index.*)

5. *Replace some titles less frequently.* Some titles may not be revised extensively enough to justify replacing them on an annual basis. Cancelling standing orders and replacing them less frequently might be considered. (Tyckoson's examples include *Annual Book of ASTM Standards* and *Diode D.A.T.A. Book.*)

6. *Cancel "spin-offs" duplicating information available in parent sources.* Some reference sources repackage information available in more comprehensive works to which the library may also subscribe. Spin-offs covering specific subject areas may be convenient, but cancelling them involves no real loss of information. (Tyckoson's examples include *Abstracts of Entomology* and *Abstracts of Health Effects of Environmental Pollutants.*)

7. *Cancel sources duplicating government publications.* The

contents of some commercially published sources duplicate government publications that may be less expensive, and that depository libraries may already be receiving free of charge. (Tyckoson's examples include *Cities of the World* and *Constitutions of the United States*.)

Electronic Reference Sources

In reviewing the reference serials collections, the library may also want to consider electronic alternatives to printed sources. Again, this is a policy issue and (unfortunately) there seems to be no clear professional consensus in this area as yet. For example, Kristine Salomon in a recent article on the impact of CD-ROM on reference departments represented a dominant point of view when she stated: "There appears to be a lack of agreement on the cancellation of printed sources with CD-ROM equivalents. Content, currency, and cost appear to be factors influencing the decision to cancel print subscriptions."[6] As more and more libraries confront serial budget deficits, however, the critical importance of the question of electronic sources in general (and for reference CD-ROM products in particular) will become even more evident. Perhaps the following statement by Ann Bristow at Indiana University summarizes the current dilemma:

> These CD-ROM sources are very basic indispensable indexes. We will wait until at least two matters are clearer before relying on CD products in place of locally owned eye-readable versions: (1) publishers' policies about what we "own" and what we are only leasing and must return at the end of the lease period and (2) standardization issues and general success of the technology which will offer the security that we will be able to 'play' disks purchased in 1988 well into 1998."[7]

CONFLICT RESOLUTION

As the above paragraphs suggest, there is likely to be some disagreement (if not outright conflict) during the course of a reference weeding project. It is realistic to expect such conflict and it would be wise to prepare for it.

Disagreements may arise within the reference department over the value/utility of certain titles. Tension may become evident when technical services staff question the processing priorities of the project. In some cases, faculty members may become involved when there is a perceived threat to a "favorite" reference source. The information contained in a "classic" reference source may be misleading or out-of-date, yet no reference collection should be without it (at least according to the faculty member).

A mechanism for dealing with such concerns should be established at the outset of the project. In most cases, the coordinating group can resolve such questions by means of a vote or through a more informal consensus process. Or, conversely, one person may be the final designated arbiter for such questions. The point is that there is in place a process for resolving these kinds of issues and guidelines to which the library can refer in making such decisions. And, of course, it helps to be flexible: one particular source will not make or break the reference collection.

Two more points need to be made with regard to the issue of resolving disagreements in the decision making process. The first is that the dual structure of the review process should guarantee that potential areas of disagreement are at least identified. In other words, each section of the reference collection receives a first and a second pass by two different individuals. It is even possible to create a "problem shelf" where final weeding decisions can be made on titles where there have been disagreements. This secondary pass or review will add to the length of the project, but is well worth the time spent.

Finally, reference librarians will probably feel more comfortable in this review process if they check their subject area or section against standard bibliographies such as Sheehy's *Guide to Reference Books* or discipline-specific bibliographies such as Lorna M. Daniells' *Business Information Sources*. Librarians will not only be able to determine superseded editions more easily, but they may also be able to identify major lacunae if they use bibliographic tools in the pruning process. Pruning, in this context, becomes a process of *subtracting* from and *adding* to the collection in order to strengthen its information use-value. Collection management thus becomes collection building, and this too can serve to mitigate concerns about the impact of weeding on a reference collection.

WRAP-UP AND CONCLUSION

Evaluation/Review

While the project should be monitored as it evolves, it is probably worthwhile to build in a more formal effort to assess the results of the weeding process at the conclusion of its implementation phase. Questions that might be addressed at this stage would include the following: (1) Was it worth the effort? If not, why not? (2) What revisions need to be made in policies/procedures/forms in order to make the next project more efficient and effective? (3) How do other departments in the library perceive the process? What adjustments need to be made in processing procedures to ensure the smooth flow of materials to their proper destinations? The evaluation process needs to be built into the project and the recommendations that emerge from it included in future efforts.

Conclusions

Most major reference review projects will take at least a year, from the initial planning to the period of review/deselection on through to the final processing of materials. It is important to recognize at the outset that there will be periods of frustration as well as periods of real achievement. This is especially the case if it happens to be the library's first reference weeding project. But it is also important to recognize that after the first time, it will become increasingly a matter of routine. Indeed, different segments or parcels of the collection can be done each year. This will put less pressure on everyone while still moving toward the goal of a more current (up-to-date) reference collection. The latter goal is, after all, instrumental to the end that we all seek: the provision of accurate information to our particular clientele.

REFERENCES

1. Gail Schlachter, "Obsolescence, Weeding, and Bibliographic Love Canals," *RQ* 28 (Fall 1988) p. 8.

2. Paul H. Mosher, "Managing Library Collections: The Process of Review and Pruning," in *Collection Development in Libraries: A Treatise*, ed. Robert D. Stueart and George B. Miller, Jr., Greenwich, CT: JAI Press, 1980, Part A, pp. 170-71.

3. Kathleen Coleman and Pauline Dickinson, "Drafting a Reference Collection Policy," *College & Research Libraries* 38 (May 1977) p. 232.

4. Coleman and Dickinson, p. 232.

5. The authors are indebted to David A. Tyckoson for these seven "Creative Journal Cancellation Ideas," contained in his paper entitled "Putting the Reference Collection on a Diet: Managing a Reference Collection Serials Cancellation Project," Poster Session paper presented at the American Library Association Annual Conference, San Francisco, California, June 27-July 2, 1987 [pp. 3-4]. We urge Mr. Tyckoson to publish the ideas set forth in this excellent poster session paper so that other reference librarians may take advantage of them.

6. Kristine Salomon, "The Impact of CD-ROM on Reference Departments," *RQ* 28 (Winter 1988) p. 204.

7. Ann Bristow, "Reference Sources on CD-ROM at Indiana University," *Electronic Library* 6 (1988) p. 28.

T - #0047 - 270225 - C0 - 212/152/10 [12] - CB - 9781560240013 - Gloss Lamination